MARXISM: PAST AND PRESENT

Also by R. N. CAREW HUNT
The Theory and Practice of Communism

R. N. CAREW HUNT

MARXISM

PAST AND PRESENT

LONDON

GEOFFREY BLES

1954

Printed in Great Britain by
Richard Clay and Company Ltd
Bungay Suffolk
for Geoffrey Bles Ltd
52 Doughty Street London WC 1

First published 1954

FOREWORD

This book is based upon a course of lectures which I had the privilege of giving in Washington during the summer of 1953 at the School of Advanced International Studies of Johns Hopkins University. Their preparation and subsequent amplification led me back to the Marxist–Leninist texts, and although the views put forward in my *Theory and Practice of Communism* (1950) still seem to me substantially correct, I feel that I should have been somewhat less indulgent to Marx and Engels had I been writing it today. Thus while it may well be that Marx believed that the dictatorship of the proletariat was compatible with democracy, as democracy is a term with many meanings and he never stated explicitly which of them he accepted, it should be pointed out that the doctrine itself is not a democratic one, that is if democracy is to be allowed any liberal content. But the ascription to Engels of a belief in democracy in this sense on the grounds of his statement that "If anything is certain, it is that our party can only come into power in the form of a democratic republic" was an error, for reasons which will be given in their place.

A re-reading of Marx's writings (with which I include those of Engels, whose modesty in assigning to his friend all that was original in their system, albeit commendable, was probably justified) inclined me to feel that there has been a tendency to treat him with too much deference. To venture such an opinion is indeed to give offence to those (and I do not refer to communists) who, while prepared to concede that he expressed himself at times with a certain lack of caution, none the less regard him as a light shining in the darkness of his generation, and the creator of a great philosophic synthesis. Undeniably he made a valuable contribution by compelling attention to the influence of economic forces upon the structure and habit of life of society, though the doctrine by which he sought to demonstrate this becomes tenable only when it has been metamorphosed into one that is no longer his own. Yet when we have to evaluate a system, it is surely permissible to judge it by what happens, or is likely to happen, when it is applied. But here Marx stands on no sure ground. His obsessional preoccupation with the French revolutionary tradition was most unfortunate, and a disservice to the genuinely progressive movement of his age. Society is totally corrupted, and must be reconstituted on an entirely new basis. The whole field of practical reform is ruled out as irrelevant to the situation. It is that fanatical type of "all-or-nothing" thinking, so characteristic of communist polemics, which first sets up an unattainable goal, and then rejects as worthless compromises whatever can be shown to fall short of it.

There are many reasons, as we shall see, why Marxism should have made so wide an appeal. Yet it is hard to be satisfied with a social analysis in which human beings do not appear as individuals, but always as collectives, formed by the class relation of their members to production, and to be judged solely by their probable reaction to a revolution. In his *Capital* Marx does indeed give many examples of the ill-usage to which the workers were subjected under the capitalist system, of which it is represented as the inevitable outcome, as when he declared in 1875, and quite wrongly, that child labour was unavoidable because the system could not get on without it. Such abuses enabled him to attack that system and predict its downfall, and there is no reason to doubt his abhorrence of them. In a letter to Engels of October 1867 he expresses his indignation at the attempt to hold up legislation based on the findings of the Children Employment Commission, which had been appointed five years earlier, and concludes, "It is a question of *abolishing the torture* of one and a half million human beings, not including the adult male working men". But his conviction that only a revolution would cure the ills of society was so absolute as to make it impossible for him to associate himself wholeheartedly with any reforming policy. As he told the Working Men's International Association in 1864, the Ten Hours Bill was "a great practical success". Yet, as he went on to point out, its real importance was that "it was the victory of a principle, the first time that in broad daylight the political economy of the middle class succumbed to the political economy of the working class". He never lost sight of the ultimate goal—the destruction of the capitalist system—and every measure of reform was to be judged by whether it brought that goal nearer by proving, as he held for example that the Co-operative movement had done, that the system was vulnerable to attack.

A circumstance which contributed to this state of mind was that, immured as he was in the British Museum, he had no contact with those whom his theories were designed to benefit, and that what he knew of their conditions was gleaned from blue-books which condemned them as strongly as he did. Had he lived among the workers, and formed his conclusions by personal observation, it may be that he would have dealt less harshly with those outcasts of society by whose sufferings Dickens was so deeply moved. As it was, he held these unfortunates to be simply the by-products of an industrialised economy, and useless at that, as they were not genuine proletarians, and thus did not possess the type of class consciousness which would turn them into suitable revolutionary material.

The same is even more true of Lenin. The necessity for

a revolution is taken for granted, and the twenty-five volumes of his writings analyse with an amazing skill well-nigh every problem to which it can give rise. Yet we search them in vain for any understanding of the real needs of those on whose behalf it would be undertaken. Workers, peasants of this kind and that, and petty bourgeois are simply the material which the revolutionary handles in his laboratory, and which he must combine in the correct proportions if he is to generate the required explosion. As for Stalin's attitude towards the "toiling masses", enough is known to make it unnecessary to pursue the matter further.

Lenin used to quote Napoleon's dictum, "On s'engage, et puis on voit". Yet while this may be an admirable maxim for a military commander who has the limited objective of winning a battle, it is very undesirable that revolutionaries should adopt it. Those who make it their business to destroy the existing social fabric must have a clear idea of what they propose to put in its place. But neither Marx nor Lenin give much thought to this matter, nor do they ever seem to have asked themselves what practical and positive advantage the ordinary citizen would derive from his "liberation". Where they should have been most explicit they fell back upon vague generalisations, and accused of "utopianism" anyone who sought to define how the society of the future would actually work. Yet this is only to be expected when any measure designed to remove a concrete evil is dismissed as "reformism" unless its removal can be shown to further the cause of revolution; and it is not surprising that the attempt to impose upon an imperfect world an order of perfect freedom, and to do so by violence, should have ended in disillusionment.

Yet human nature is so constituted that a doctrine which appeals to hatred and class warfare has exerted, and continues to exert, considerable influence. As soon, indeed, as that doctrine is subjected to analysis its theoretical inadequacy becomes apparent, and that it has been so often exposed may seem to require an apology for treading once again so well-worn a path. But as long as it is proclaimed and finds adherents, those who do not agree with it may be allowed to state their reasons. I have sought therefore to re-examine the basic concepts of revolutionary Marxism, and to show in what respects they have been modified. I have chosen my title because it is the simplest expression of what I want to write about; but I should make clear that when I speak of Marxism in the present, I mean Moscow's interpretation of it. In the text I have found it convenient, however, to refer upon occasions to those who subscribe to this interpretation as Marxist–Leninists—the term ordinarily employed today to denote those who accept Marx's teaching as elaborated by Lenin and Stalin.

I acknowledge with gratitude my debt to those to whose assistance I owe so much, and in particular to Professor K. R. Popper, Mr. Isaiah Berlin, Mr. J. P. Mayer, Mr. L. B. Schapiro, Mr. E. E. Orchard and Mr. H. J. Blackham. I am under an especial obligation to Professor H. B. Acton, who not only read the whole typescript but also helped me with many valuable suggestions. For the views expressed in the book, and for its shortcomings, I must take the responsibility.

R. N. CAREW HUNT

May, 1954

CONTENTS

Introduction

The Marxist system, which forms the basis of the present communist creed, professes to account for the various forms which society has assumed, and to show that the operation of the laws which allegedly govern its development must ultimately bring into existence a communist society. At the centre of the system is the doctrine of historical materialism, since all the elements of the Marxist political, social and economic theory are either contained in it, or are held to follow inevitably from its premises. If there is any single phrase which sums up Marx's teaching it is the famous apostrophe at the end of the *Theses on Feuerbach*, "Hitherto philosophers have sought to interpret the world; the point, however, is to change it". This is what communists have ever since attempted to do. But to change the world, by which is meant human society, since even communists do not set out to remove mountains in the literal sense, there must be an understanding of its nature. It is this that historical materialism professes to supply. It is the communist philosophy of history in so far as it is the purpose of such philosophies to account for why the development of a particular civilisation or period took the form it did, and thus perhaps offer some guidance as to what we may ourselves expect in the future. As such, it has gained a wider acceptance than any rival explanation advanced in modern times, and has brought about, as Engels claimed, a revolution in the social sciences comparable to that which Darwin effected in the natural sciences. It provided the basis of what became known in the last century as "scientific socialism"— scientific because of Marx's demonstration that socialism is a determined historic form of society which becomes necessary when production has reached a certain stage of development. This was felt at the time to be a more effective explanation of social change than that advanced by the so-called "Utopian Socialists", who had based their systems upon concepts of morality and justice which, Engels observed, "do not take us an inch further"; and thus in one western European country after another socialist parties arose which based their programmes upon it.

What was not sufficiently recognised, however, in these early years was that historical materialism was by no means as straightforward and axiomatic as had been at first supposed. Not only was it disquieting that so many of its major predictions should have failed to stand up to the test of time, but when this led to a closer enquiry, it was found unexpectedly difficult to be certain of its precise meaning. For although Marx and Engels were prolific writers, no single work of theirs contains a complete exposition of it, and the Italian Socialist, Antonio Labriola, was the first to set it out in a systematic form.[1] It is to be found in embryo in Marx's early philosophic writings; its main theses are stated in the *Communist Manifesto*; Marx's *Eighteenth Brumaire* first attempted to apply it to a current political situation; it is formulated concisely but all too briefly in the preface to his *Critique of Political Economy*; and there are repeated references to it in his *Capital*. The best account of it is, however, in Engels' *The Origin of the Family* and his *Anti-Dühring*, and the last-named contributed more than any other of their joint writings to making it generally known.

In his speech at Marx's graveside, Engels, who knew him better than any man, declared that, "Before all else, Marx was a great revolutionist", and the same was equally true of himself. There is therefore a certain ambivalence in their writings. They purport to be objective

[1] B. Croce, "Come nacque e come mori' il Marxismo", *Critica*, 1938, p. 43. The reference is to Labriola's *Del materialismo storico*, 1896.

studies of the facts, while at the same time they are dooms upon existing society, exploding its pretensions and crying out for its destruction. Hence the standard by which strictly scientific treatises should be judged is not entirely applicable to them. Yet both men would have felt seriously affronted had they been told that their conclusions would be tested by any other. They regarded themselves as social scientists, and as they claimed that what they called "our theory" had for the first time revealed the true nature of social reality, we must take them at their own valuation.

Sidney Hook has observed, however, that the trouble with "scientific socialism" was not that it was scientific, but that it was not scientific enough. Neither Marx nor Engels were at sufficient pains to define the terms they used or, if they did so, to stick to their definitions; so that we find Marx devoting the three great volumes of his *Capital* to analysing the concept of value without ever making clear what he meant by it.[1] Nor is this all. With the passage of time their early revolutionary writings became outdated by events, as they themselves occasionally admitted—particularly Engels in the prefaces he wrote to the later editions of Marx's works. Yet they made little attempt to restate their doctrine, and allowed it to be understood that in its main lines it still held good. The form which Lenin was to give it, and which Stalin inherited, was naturally influenced by the problems raised by the October revolution, and this has become the orthodox form which is accepted by communists in all countries. Yet it was a legitimate interpretation of principles, which had never been disavowed. That their application should have led to a police state is only what might have been expected, though it is doubtful whether, at the time of the revolution, Lenin and the other Bolshevik leaders foresaw this development or intended it to take place.

[1] A. Gray, *The Socialist Tradition*, 1946, p. 321.

"I hope", says Engels, "that even British respectability will not be over-shocked if I use the term 'historical materialism' to designate that view of the course of history which seeks the ultimate cause and the great moving power of all important historic events in the economic development of society, in the changes in the modes of production and exchange, in the consequent division of society into distinct classes, and in the struggles of these classes against one another."[1] Yet Eduard Bernstein holds "the economic interpretation of history" to be a more suitable designation, as it avoids the problems associated with philosophical materialism which have no relevance to Marx's thesis;[2] though, against this, it has been pointed out that such a designation implies that there are other ways in which it is permissible to interpret history, which communists deny.[3] Kautsky agrees that the introduction of "materialism" is to be regretted, and prefers "economic determinism", a term favoured by French writers, but which confronts us with the question as to what "determinism" means,[4] Croce calls it the "realist interpretation of history". It is not a new methodology, and is simply a canon of interpretation which directs our attention to the economic basis of society.[5] On the other hand, Max Adler regards it as an heuristic principle only. It provides the basis for the scientific treatment of history. More than this it does not do, and its connection with materialism is to be rejected, since materialism involves the problem of the nature of matter and of its relation to mind, with which science has nothing to do, as it is concerned with the causal relation between phenomena and not

[1] Introduction to the 1892 English edition of *Socialism: Utopian and Scientific*, Marx–Engels, (S)elected (W)orks = S.W., II, p. 94.
[2] *Die Voraussetzungen des Sozialismus*, 1899, Eng. trans. *Evolutionary Socialism*, 1909, pp. 17–19.
[3] Charles Turgeon, *Critique de la conception matérialiste de l'histoire*, Paris, 1930, p. 16.
[4] *Die materialistische Geschichtsauffassung*, Berlin, 1927, I, pp. 19 f.
[5] *Historical Materialism and the Teaching of Karl Marx*, Eng. trans. 1914, p. 77.

with their nature, and whether they are material or spiritual or a combination of both is a matter of indifference.[1] Similar differences of opinion have persisted down to our own day, but the above will be sufficient to indicate their general trend.

None the less, the term "historical materialism", which Engels adopted, is to be preferred because, albeit the really significant element in the Marxist system, it cannot be dissociated from the larger philosophy of dialectical materialism of which it is a particular application. The argument that Marx could have said all he wanted to say without introducing the dialectic at all is irrelevant even if it were true. He deliberately chose to make use of it because it seemed to him the most convenient way of accounting for progress in society, and his doctrine cannot be fully understood without it. He may indeed have had little interest in extending it to cover all phenomena —a task undertaken by Engels and pursued by Lenin. Yet once it is accepted as inherent in any one aspect of reality, it is hard to see upon what grounds its inherence in reality as a whole can be denied. Moreover, his is a *total* system—one in which all human thought and action are related to a single determining principle. But the search for this principle compelled him to enquire into the nature of reality and of man as a part of reality, and so create a philosophic basis for his theory of society. Thus although it is with this theory that we are primarily concerned, his philosophy of dialectical materialism must be our starting point, just as it was his own.[2] We have therefore to ask what is meant by the two terms of this strange hybrid. They present different problems, and require separate treatment.

---

[1] *Lehrbuch der materialistische Geschichtsauffassung*, Basle, 1930, p. 18.

[2] It is, however, of interest to note that although Marx and Engels have much to say about the application of the dialectic to material phenomena, neither of them actually use the term "dialectical materialism", which seems first to have been employed by Plekhanov, and was to be given an even wider currency by Lenin.

I

Dialectics

Marx's early philosophical studies brought him into conflict with two schools—the eighteenth-century French materialists, of whom he takes Hélvetius and Holbach as representative, and contemporary German idealist philosophy, of which Hegel was at that time the most prominent exponent. He rejected them both, though his own system was a combination of elements borrowed from each. In his *Holy Family* he admitted that the French materialists had rendered good service, particularly by attacking religion. But their outlook had been mechanistic because it was based on the dominant science of their day—mechanics, the science of moving bodies. In their view, all that existed were material particles, each separate and independent, and these particles interacted through the impulsion of external forces. The world was thus a complicated machine which required to be set going, but thereafter acted in accordance with laws that could be exactly stated. The objection to this was first, that if the world was a machine, there must have been some "prime mover" who started it upon its course, and that this opened the way to belief in a Supreme Being, on whose existence most members of this school were in fact agreed; and secondly, that while such a conception could account for differences caused by race, geographical conditions and the like, it contained no explanation of change in the sense of progress, since, as Cornforth puts it, "Just as a machine has to be wound up, so it will only do what it is meant to do. It cannot change itself or produce any new quality." [1]

[1] Maurice Cornforth, *Dialectical Materialism*, 1952, p. 44.

The French materialists applied the same mechanical conception to human nature. It was, they held, neither good nor bad, but a plastic substance, which was moulded into the form it assumed by education, laws and institutions—agencies external to man, whose function it was to bring about social harmony. It is true that their demand for changes in existing education, laws and institutions led them to advocate far-reaching programmes of reform, and for this they were to be commended. None the less, their view of human nature was inadequate. It exhibited men as formed by the circumstances of their environment instead of as creating this environment for themselves; while it represented society as ultimately governed by ideas, that is, by those of the moralists, legislators and other persons competent to direct the dispositions of men towards the common good, though it failed to explain why one set of ideas rather than another should be held at any particular time.[1]

German philosophy influenced Marx first through Hegel, and then through Feuerbach, who broke away from Hegel's idealism. Hegel shared the belief of the French revolutionaries in the power of reason, and his system was an attempt to demonstrate that reason governs reality. Into that system the idea of creative evolution enters as a fundamental principle, since it insists that reality is not static but dynamic, and that it can be understood only in terms of becoming, not of being. This led him to assert the existence of a dialectical principle in accordance with which any complex of phenomena, such as those which constitute a civilisation, will inevitably develop contradictions which are inherent in its very nature. These contradictions, respectively the thesis and the antithesis, will then give rise to a conflict in which they will become reconciled in a synthesis on a higher level, because the reconciliation will take the form of uniting what is worth preserving in

[1] J. L. Talmon, *The Origins of Totalitarian Democracy*, 1952, pp. 33–34.

7

each. Yet this synthesis is not final, and will lead in due course to new conflicts which will be similarly resolved. It is this unending process of conflict and reconciliation which is at once the cause and the explanation of change and development.

Hegel's conception of the dialectic is therefore that of a logic which transcends formal logic and has become an ontology because it offers its principles as universal laws which explain the nature of reality. Hegel concedes, as do Marxist–Leninists today, that formal logic possesses a certain limited value, but both argue that it can only be applied to things which are at rest, and that it breaks down as soon as an attempt is made to apply it to things which are in process of development. Thus the *Short Philosophic Dictionary*, edited by M. Rozenthal and P. F. Yudin in 1939, of which there have been numerous revisions, declares that it played an important part in the seventeenth and eighteenth centuries, when sciences in the modern sense were being created. These sciences investigated phenomena in terms of their independence of one another rather than in terms of their interconnection, an approach which was in keeping with the limitations of this type of logic.[1] But for this very reason it is inadequate. It is in fact essentially a "bourgeois logic", because the bourgeoisie is always fearful of change which would destroy it as a class, and is thus forever seeking to establish principles which are represented as unchanging.[2]

Hence, according to the dialecticians, once reality is conceived as dynamic it becomes impossible to apply to it the laws of formal logic, viz. the Law of Identity (that $A = A$), the Law of Contradiction (that a thing cannot be at the same time A and non-A), and the Law of the Excluded Middle (that a thing is either A or non-A). For

---

[1] See under *Formal Logic* in Howard Selsam's adaptation of the 1940 edition of the dictionary entitled *Handbook of Philosophy*, New York, 1949.
[2] Cornforth, *op. cit.*, p. 37.

these laws Hegel therefore substituted the three laws of the dialectic, viz. the Law of the Unity of Opposites (or, alternatively, of the Identity of Contradictions), which asserts that opposites or contradictions do not exclude but mutually imply one another; the Law of the Negation of the Negation, according to which the conflict between two opposites or contradictions (the thesis and the anti-thesis) must result in a higher synthesis (the negation of the negation); and the Law of the Transformation of Quantity into Quality, which insists that change takes place as a result of a series of quantitative mutations which continue until a point is reached when a new quality emerges. The dialectic is thus the conflict and reconciliation of opposites or contradictions producing progress.[1]

The above criticism, and the laws in which it is ex-pressed, rest, however, on a misapprehension of the func-tion of logic. It is not concerned to explain the nature of reality, but with the argumentative aspect of thought. Once this is understood, the objections raised against it by dialecticians break down. They maintain that the hard-and-fast distinctions of formal logic do not find their counterpart in reality. But even if this were always true, it would be irrelevant. What formal logic asserts is that if we are thinking about something, we must be consistent and not use the same symbol in different senses; that if we assume, as we are perfectly entitled to do, a division be-tween that which is A and that which is not-A, we cannot say that a thing is both at once at the same time and in the same respect; and that, again assuming such a divi-sion, a thing must be either A or not-A and there is no third alternative.[2] It should be noted that the denial of this last proposition is inconsistent, as Hook points out,

---

[1] F. J. Sheed, *Communism and Man*, 1938, p. 6.
[2] Alexander Philipov, *Logic and Dialectic in the Soviet Union*, New York, 1952, p. 31.

with the Marxist view that at the major turning points of history society has been confronted with only two possible alternatives, so that Engels repeatedly stated that in modern times there was no choice between socialism and capitalism.[1] The same argument has been used in communist propaganda of recent years against those social-democratic politicians who have advocated a "third-force" policy, which would oppose equally Soviet communism and American imperialism.

How was it, then, that Hegel came to hold this view? It was because, in his system, the Idea (which is reason or pure thought) is identified with reality, so that everything within reality must be subject to the laws which govern the Idea. He then shows that the Idea unfolds itself and comes to complete self-consciousness through a process which is dialectical because it takes place through the conflict of opposite or contradictory categories and their reconciliation on a higher plane—a conflict for which he uses the thesis, antithesis and synthesis as symbols. Here we have indeed a principle of development, but the factors in the process are categories of thought interacting according to a strictly logical pattern, which is reasonable once it is assumed that the Idea is identical with reality. It should be observed, however, that in his *Logic* Hegel did not reject the Law of Contradiction, and that he regarded contradictions as necessarily entering into the process of thinking, as we discover for ourselves when we try to reconcile in our minds two conflicting points of view. But his identification of the Idea with reality led him to conclude that the contradictions that arise in thought are due to contradictions in being, and therein lies the paradox. It is perfectly intelligible that we should think of a thing as black from one point of view and not black from another, and such a contradiction may be reconciled. But it is quite another thing to argue, as he does, that the

---

[1] *Reason, Social Myths and Reality*, New York, 1940, p. 187.

reason we do this is because the thing itself is black and at the same time not black.[1]

What therefore Hegel did was to construct a reality of his own in which the dialectic was the moving force so that it became the explanation of all development within reality. Marx did the same thing. He condemned the French materialists because he could find in their system no principle which would account for development in history. At the same time, he condemned Hegel for identifying the Idea with reality, but took over his dialectic as providing him with the dynamic principle he needed. Thus, the position he reached was dialectical materialism. Social reality is not the Idea, but material economic forces; but these forces possess the property of developing in accordance with the laws that govern the Idea, that is, with the laws of thought which Hegel had shown to be dialectical. In an often-quoted passage in the preface to the second edition of his *Capital* he explains that the "arrogance and mediocrity" of contemporary German philosophers had led him "to avow himself a pupil of Hegel", and that he had "even here and there coquetted with the modes of expression peculiar to him". In fact, he accepted the dialectic as completely as he rejected the rest of Hegel's system. He had, he declared, found him on his head, and had set him the right way up, though what he had actually done was to restore the dialectic to the form it had originally assumed in German philosophy—that of a philosophy of nature—before Hegel turned it upside down by giving it an idealist form.[2] Engels shared his enthusiasm. The dialectic, he insisted, is "our best working tool, our sharpest instrument".[3] The greatest merit of the school culminating with Hegel had been its re-adoption as "the highest form of thinking", and he noted that he and

[1] Paul Foulquié, *La Dialectique*, Paris, 1949, pp. 53–55.
[2] H. A. Hodges, "The Thought of Karl Marx" in *Christian Faith and Communist Faith*, 1953, p. 11.
[3] *Feuerbach*, S.W., II, p. 350.

Marx had been "pretty well the only people to rescue [it] from German idealist philosophy and apply it in the materialist conception of nature and of history".[1] And again, "Without German philosophy, particularly that of Hegel, German scientific socialism, the only scientific socialism that has ever existed, would never have come into being".[2]

It is sometimes suggested that all Marx and Engels were concerned to do was to protest against the practice adopted by many of their contemporaries of treating social and economic phenomena as a part of the natural order, and thus unchangeable; and that as they had been brought up in the Hegelian tradition, they used the dialectic in order to do this. There is indeed at all times a tendency for thinkers to hold that the eternal nature of such concepts as they particularly cherish is in some way guaranteed, and here Marxist–Leninists themselves form no exception. Yet even when Marx and Engels were young men, the notion of evolution, as this is understood by scientists, was not a new one, and if they had merely wished to assert that the phenomena in which they were interested were subject to change, they could well have done so without introducing the elaborate logical apparatus of the dialectic. Hook has pointed out that Engels uses the dialectic in at least seven different senses, not every one of which is compatible with the others;[3] and although he seems ultimately to have understood by it the rhythm of things in their development, it also had for him other implications. That development is dialectical and not simply evolutionary is a part of the Marxist–Leninist creed, and thus all evolutionary theories are condemned as inadequate, including Darwinism, although this had provided, as Marx puts it, "the basis in natural history for our

---

[1] *Anti-Dühring*, p. 26.
[2] Preface to *The Peasant War in Germany*, [S]elected [W]orks, ed. 1950, I, p. 590.
[3] "Dialectic and Nature" in *Reason, Social Myths and Democracy*, pp. 183 f.

theory".[1] But in fact Marx and Engels were looking for a principle which would uphold a doctrine of revolution rather than of evolution, and it was because the dialectic appeared to do this that they incorporated it into their system.

Yet neither had any justification at all for using it, as it only makes sense in terms of thought. In Hegel's system it has a place. But there are no grounds for supposing that material phenomena exhibit in their change and development the same process of logical inter-relation as that which governs the Idea. What Marxist–Leninists do, however, is arbitrarily to select any two dissimilar phenomena, and then represent them as logical contradictions to which the laws of the dialectic apply, thus contravening the principle of formal logic that while propositions and statements may be contradictory, things and events cannot be.[2] When, however, the German social-democrat, Eugen Dühring, accused Marx of being unable to prove his theory of social development without having recourse to the "artifices" and "fantasies" of the Hegelian dialectic, Engels replied that Marx was simply arguing from historical data. "The process is an historical one, and if at the same time it is a dialectical process, this is not Marx's fault." All he had done had been to show that a certain process had occurred in the past and must occur in the future, and to characterise it as one which took place in accordance with the laws of the dialectic.[3]

This defence is altogether disingenuous. Certainly when Marx first came to set out his doctrine of historical materialism, his approach was a positivist one, that is, he held that that alone is knowledge which is perceived through the senses or revealed through the natural sciences, and that it was thus possible to construct a science of society upon an empirical basis. Yet his method

[1] Marx to Engels, Dec. 19, 1860, *Correspondence*, ed. Dona Torr, 1934, p. 126.
[2] Hook, *op. cit.*, p. 202.   [3] *Anti-Dühring*, p. 152.

is not inductive but dialectical, and though he appeals to the facts, it is to support conclusions which go far beyond what is empirically demonstrable. In any case, belief in the dialectic is incompatible with empiricism. The empiricist must be prepared to admit that he may be mistaken, and thus the communist would be obliged to recognise the possibility that some complex of phenomena may arise to which the dialectic will not apply. Marxist–Leninist theory will make no such admission.

Marx had early rejected metaphysics as idle speculation, incapable of giving genuine knowledge of reality. His followers have accepted this, and represent metaphysics and dialectics as in absolute opposition. The former, it is maintained, conceives of phenomena as possessing fixed properties and as isolated from one another, so that their relation is one of irreconcilable antitheses; whereas dialectics conceives them as inter-connected (whether physically or causally is not explained), and as in a continual state of change. But this change, which is due to contradictions inherent in their nature, does not take place through a simple process of growth, but by sudden "leaps" which bring into existence new qualities. Thus the dialectic is a universal law immanent in reality, in accordance with which lower forms are transformed into higher. By reason of its universality, it governs and explains progress within society, so that it confers upon those initiated into its processes a sort of gnosis which enables them to discern what is hidden from the mere observer of events, and in the power of this knowledge to transform the world.

Thus the Marxist dialectic leads to "historicism"—to the belief that there is a pattern in history, and that once we have discovered what it is we can not only interpret the past, but also predict the future. "Did not the theory of Marx", asks Plekhanov, "provide him with an astonishing, previously unknown, capacity to foretell events?" [1] It

[1] *In Defence of Materialism*, ed. 1947, p. 225.

is no disparagement of Marx's contribution to social theory to say that it did nothing of the kind, and that his prophecies were almost always wrong. Yet the illusion is still maintained. *The Short History of the C.P.S.U.*—Stalin's version of Marxism–Leninism under the guise of history—declares that "the power of the Marxist-Lenist theory lies in the fact that it enables the party to find the right orientation in any situation, to understand the inner connection of current events, to foresee their course, and to perceive not only how they are developing in the present, but how and in what direction they are bound to develop in the future".[1] Exactly how the leaders use this invaluable instrument is not stated, and indeed nothing could be more undialectical than the hard-and-fast antitheses of their directives, as set out for example in the Cominform Journal. Yet these directives purport to be based upon a dialectical analysis of the class forces, since, as Lenin declared, "We Marxists have always been proud of the fact that by a strict analysis of the mass forces and mutual class relations we have been able to determine the expediency of this or that form of mass struggle".[2] In this event, it is singular that the party theoreticians should so often have reached completely opposed conclusions. But they are handicapped by starting from certain presuppositions which are not merely working hypotheses to be discarded if subsequently ascertained facts fail to support them, but revealed truths to which the facts must be made to conform. Thus they are obliged to declare that the capitalist system is everywhere disintegrating and that the workers are increasingly exploited under it, not because there is any evidence for either, but because the dialectic requires it, so that all it does is to prevent them from looking at what they pretend to describe.

[1] p. 355.
[2] "On the Revolutionary Phase", *Pravda*, Feb. 21, 1918; *Works*, 3rd Russian ed. XXII, p. 265. For an example of how such an analysis should be carried out see *Left-Wing Communism and Infantile Disorder*, S.W., X, p. 137.

At the same time, the extravagant claims made for the dialectic should not blind us to the fact that it does provide an interesting approach to history, and that when Lenin exclaimed to Maxim Gorky, "By gad, the philosopher Hegel was right—life does proceed by contradictions", he was not simply talking nonsense.[1] To represent it as a supreme law governing all phenomena is absurd, and even more so to suppose that it is an infallible guide to an understanding of every historical situation, which the innumerable blunders of Soviet policy sufficiently disprove. Yet, as has been pointed out by K.R. Popper—no friend to the dialectic, whether that of Hegel or of Marx —it does provide "a fairly good description" of certain developments, especially of the development of ideas and theories and of movements based upon them. It emphasises that although a theory may be proved wrong, it is likely to contain something worth preserving or it would never have been taken seriously. Only, he adds, we must not say that a thesis "produces" its antithesis, since the conflict is one which only arises because our minds have become aware of it, and if the critical faculty is lacking it will not take place. Nor is it true to say that the conflict between the thesis and the antithesis always leads to a synthesis. It may lead to nothing, as many examples show. The only "force" which may promote a dialectical development is our critical attitude, that is, our reluctance to accept contradictions either between a theory and a statement of fact or between two theories, and thus look for a new starting point which will enable us to avoid them. This reluctance is expressed in formal logic by the Law of Contradiction, which asserts that a contradiction is unacceptable because it must always be false; and the refusal to accept this law destroys the basis of criticism, and with it the whole "dialectical" process. The advance

[1] Letter of Nov. 27, 1909, quoted by Edmund Walsh, *Total Empire*, Milwaukee, 1951, pp. 108–109.

16

of science depends upon the discovery of contradictions in our theories and their removal. Once the law is denied, the discovery ceases to have any importance.[1]

But for Marxist–Leninists the force behind the dialectic is a tension within phenomena themselves, which leads to conflict, and through conflict to development. The dialectic has thus provided the communist movement with its *mystique*. It is to the indoctrinated party member rather what Providence is to the believing Christian—that to which all things are subject, and in accordance with which they work to their appointed ends. Thus the communist holds that behind the flux of day-to-day events a struggle is going on, the true nature of which is revealed only to the initiated. It is a struggle between two forces, one of which is dying while the other is coming to birth, and it is working itself out inexorably according to a law which possesses the same validity as the laws which govern the natural sciences, and which ensures the victory of the new and emergent force over that which is old and decaying. In that struggle everyone must take a side, and indeed is doing so whether he is aware of it or not. He is either supporting the force which has history on its side, or that on which history has passed judgement. There can be no middle course.

The dialectic thus guarantees the eventual transition of society into communism, because communism is the only logical outcome of the contradictions to which every other economic system gives rise. In this event, it might be expected that communists would passively await this inevitable consummation, whereas in fact they do nothing of the sort. How far a process which is working itself out inexorably in history can be influenced by human activity is a question we shall have to consider later. Here we need only note that the classless society of communism is simply the contemporary expression of that belief in a

[1] "What is Dialectic?", *Mind*, 1940, pp. 105–107.

pre-ordained and natural order of justice which will introduce harmony into society which, as J. L. Talmon has
shown in his *Origins of Totalitarian Democracy*, was held by
the more liberal-minded French political thinkers of
the eighteenth century, and was identified by Rousseau
with the "general will". This blue-print of social justice
possesses for communists an absolute value, and thus any
means are justified which will bring it into existence. As
they hold, moreover, that the dialectic alone gives knowledge which is certain, it is impossible for them to admit
that any views can be correct which are contrary to their
own. If therefore any group rejects their policies once
these have been explained to them, it can only be because
its members are inspired by interests which are contrary
to those of the people, of whom it must therefore be
accounted the enemy. Marxism–Leninism fails in fact to
provide a theory of uncertain judgements, and to allow
for situations in which any one of a number of different
views may reasonably be held on the evidence available.

Yet the laws of the dialectic are no longer invoked to
justify this way of thinking in the form in which they used
to be. Current expositions of Marxism–Leninism scarcely
mention the Law of the Negation of the Negation, though
without it the dialectic fails to provide an explanation of
development, and both Marx and Engels had appealed
to it, the latter describing it as "an extremely general . . .
and for this reason an extremely important law of
development of nature, history and thought".[1] But both
Plekhanov and Lenin had warned against the employment of the Hegelian triad, doubtless because contemporary Marxists were applying it in such a way as to
expose the whole system to ridicule.[2] In his *Concerning
Marxism in Linguistics* (1950) Stalin declared that the Law

---

[1] *Anti-Dühring*, p. 159.
[2] *In Defence of Materialism*, pp. 99–100, 248; *What "The Friends of the
People" Are*, S.W., I, pp. 102–103.

of the Transformation of Quantity into Quality, which had hitherto provided the dialectical explanation of the inevitability of revolution, applied only to changes within class-divided societies, thus denying to the law its universal character.[1] There only remains, therefore, the Law of the Union of Opposites, which asserts that contradictions are always reconcilable, and which is retained because it can be used to justify any inconsistencies, however blatant.

[1] pp. 19–21.

II

Materialism

The materialist side of the Marxist–Leninist philosophy confronts us with a further set of difficulties. Materialism is ordinarily understood to be the assertion that everything is ultimately reducible to material terms, and Marxist–Leninists insist that Marx's great discovery was the dependence of mind upon the external world. But he was not in fact concerned with materialism in this sense. His materialism is anti-idealism, and the position he is refuting is that which only admits the reality of mind. It is true that this led him to view with suspicion any attempt to postulate a spiritual principle independent of matter, and to use language which can be interpreted as denying the existence of such a principle. It is also true that the implications of his doctrine of historical materialism are grossly materialistic. Yet although he probably shared the materialist views which passed current in his day, his writings do not commit him to more than realism—the position which asserts that material phenomena exist in their own right, leaving it an open question whether there may not be other phenomena which are not material.

Engels, however, went further than this, and when Lenin formulated what was to become the official philosophy, it was to him that he turned rather than to Marx. For in his *Feuerbach*, Engels lays down that "materialism regards the concepts in our heads as images (*Abbilder*) of real things, instead of regarding the real things as images of this or that state of development of an absolute concept".[1] This again is directed against ideal-

[1] S.W., II, p. 350: cp. Lenin, *Materialism and Empirio-criticism*, 1908, S.W., XI, pp. 108–109.

ism, and represents a position that anyone might hold without calling it materialism. But D. J. B. Hawkins points out that when Engels examines in his *Feuerbach* the relation between consciousness and being, he confuses two problems which are quite distinct—that of knowledge and that of the nature of reality. As to the first, he is a realist. We must start with the facts, and their existence is presupposed by our awareness of them. In this sense it is true to say that being determines consciousness rather than the other way round. But he then goes on to declare that mind is simply a product of matter, and to censure Feuerbach for admitting as much and then denying that he was a materialist. It is not to be supposed that Engels was simply enunciating the truism that brains cannot exist without bodies. What he meant was that all being is fundamentally material. But this is to say much more than that consciousness presupposes being, and it commits him to materialism.[1]

As for the nature of matter, Engels explains in his *Dialectics of Nature* that "once we have come to know the forms of the motion of matter, we have come to know what matter is and have exhausted the knowledge of it". Only by "motion" he does not simply mean transposition in space, as he points out that in dialectical materialism it means "change in general", but that this change takes place according to the laws of the dialectic, that is, within a unity of which all the elements are inter-connected, and not as a result of the impact upon these elements of any external force. Thus the term "motion" is first interpreted as "change", and "change" as a "creative activity" which produces new qualities. This "creative activity" is then represented as an historical process. Such a conception of motion is foreign to earlier forms of materialism. But if there was to be any progress within a purely material

[1] "The Philosophical Background of Marx and Engels", *Blackfriars*, Feb. 1953, pp. 57–58.

universe, matter had to be endowed with the property of creative activity. The trouble is that by the time it has been so endowed it has ceased to be matter.

Similarly, Lenin declares that "there is nothing in the world except matter and its motion". But if matter is all that exists, there can be no means of defining it, as it can possess no characteristic which distinguishes it from something else, seeing that this something else can only be non-existence.[1] Lenin maintains, however, that it stands in no need of definition because, for the philosopher, it is simply that which, operating upon our sense organs, creates experience, and this holds good whatever scientists may have to say about its nature. According to the Soviet theoretician, M. Mitin, all that dialectical materialism demands of its votaries is that they should recognise the existence of an objective world independent of mind.[2] Yet Lenin was not content with this position. His treatment of materialism reveals the same confusion as we have noted in the case of Engels. He too starts as a realist, concerned only to refute idealism, and then, as if without realising what he is doing, slides off into materialism by declaring that "beyond the 'physical' external world with which everyone is familiar there can be nothing".

It is, however, essential to the dialectical materialist doctrine that matter should possess the property of motion, and, according to the Law of the Union of Opposites, it is the conflict between them which causes it, and thus leads them to unite. But, as we have seen, the activity which effects their union cannot be an extrinsic force, and must be contained within the opposites themselves. Hence, as C. J. McFadden points out, their union must either be due to a basic source of motion which is common to them both, or each must possess its own auto-dynamic

---

[1] N. O. Lossky, *History of Russian Philosophy*, New York, 1951, p. 349.
[2] "Forty Years of Lenin's Empirio-criticism", *Cominform Journal*, May 15, 1949.

principle. Yet the law fails equally to account for the presence of motion within the basic source or for its presence within the opposites.[1] Berdyaev rightly argues that a philosophy which recognises the self-movement of matter, however incapable it is of explaining it, cannot be regarded as materialist; but this is only another way of saying that one which takes its stand on strictly materialist premises, as does contemporary Marxism–Leninism, has no right to talk about the self-movement of matter.[2]

Both Engels and Lenin maintain, therefore, that there exists on the one hand the material world which provides the objective conditions of knowledge and, on the other, the images in our minds which are accurate reflections of this reality. But here they are simply asserting what it is their business to prove, for if all that we are aware in consciousness are only copies, and it is impossible to compare these copies with the originals, how can there be any assurance that the two are identical? [3] Yet it is a fundamental assumption of Marxism–Leninism that we do obtain through our senses a real knowledge of the external world, and that to question this is to fall into the heresy of idealism, which, in some form or other, makes mind independent of matter, and may thus lead to belief in a creative intelligence, and even to belief in God. It is the belief that the material world exists objectively and independently of the perceiving mind that Lenin defends so passionately in his *Materialism and Empirio-criticism*. Mach and Avenarius, against whom this work was primarily directed, held the position known as phenomenalism, which maintains that it is impossible to have knowledge of anything beyond what is experienced in perception, and that the idea that there is something unex-

---

[1] *The Philosophy of Communism*, New York, 1938, pp. 176 f.
[2] *Royaume de l'Esprit et Royaume de César*, Paris, 1951, p. 127.
[3] Gustav A. Wetter, *Der dialektistische Materialismus*, Vienna, 1952, p. 491.

perienced which causes perception is absurd.[1] But Lenin held that "the existence of matter does not depend upon sensation",[2] for if it did, the logical outcome would be solipsism, the view that we only know our subjective states but cannot know what causes them, which may be something entirely different from what we experience. He therefore contended that we do in fact act consistently on the assumption that the material world is real, and that the effect of the contrary assumption would be to divorce theory from practice.

Not unnaturally, Marxist–Leninist theoreticians have proved unequal to the task of fitting the dialectic into the materialist framework. Engels had laid down in his *Anti-Dühring* that "modern materialism is essentially dialectical and no longer needs any philosophy standing above the other sciences. . . . What still independently survives of all forms of philosophy is the science of thought and its laws, formal logic and dialectics. Everything else is merged in the positive science of nature and history." [3] This view, which is not far removed from positivism, was adopted in the twenties by the so-called Mechanist group of theoreticians, under Nicolai Bukharin, in the controversy which arose between them and a second group, of which the leader was A. M. Deborin. The Mechanists threw their emphasis upon materialism, and either rejected philosophy outright, or identified it with "the ultimate conclusions of science"; to which the Deborinists retorted by stressing the dialectic, which they formulated in excessively schematic and abstract terms. Deborin was so far successful as to procure the condemnation of the Mechanists in 1929, but in 1931 his own school was also condemned, apparently on the initiative of Stalin, who

---

[1] H. B. Acton, "The Marxist Outlook", *Philosophy*, Nov. 1947, pp. 210 f. See also Alfred Fuchs, "The Development of Idealist Philosophy from Mach to Heidegger", *Modern Quarterly*, 1949–1950, pp. 225 f.

[2] S.W., XI, pp. 121–122.

[3] p. 32; cp. *Feuerbach*, S.W., II, p. 363.

wanted the philosophers to get on with the first Five-Years Plan, and regarded Deborin's system as altogether unsuitable for this purpose. In fact, the indictment of him rested upon a number of charges which bore little relation to the main issue, as for example his alleged exaltation of Plekhanov at the expense of Lenin, and the essential elements of his system found their way back into what was to become the official philosophy. This was now restated by a third group, headed by Mitin and Yudin, which attempted to reconcile the two positions by maintaining that the various sciences were autonomous, inasmuch as each possessed its own laws, but that the laws themselves were subject in turn to those general principles to which the term "dialectical" had now come to be applied. The controversy was the last occasion upon which Soviet philosophers were permitted to express their views freely, and they have since as far as possible restricted themselves to problems for which official solutions exist.[1] In 1938 there appeared Stalin's *Dialectical and Historical Materialism*, and in 1939 the *Short Philosophic Dictionary*, and it is doubtful if any statement in the field of Marxist–Leninist theory has since been made which is not contained in one or the other.

[1] On the controversy, see Wetter, *op. cit.*, pp. 159 f.; I. M. Bochenski, *Die sowjetrussische dialektische Materialismus*, Berne, 1949, pp. 48–51; P. C. Hubatka, *Die materialistische Geschichtsauffassung*, Rorschach, 1941, p. 21, n. 57.

III

Feuerbach and "True Humanism"

Hegel's system is a philosophy of the Absolute, and at the same time one in which reality is conceived as in a continual state of becoming. Much depends therefore upon which of the two elements the stress is laid. If it is upon the rationality of the actually real, the system may become a justification of the *status quo* and a philosophy of conservatism; whereas if it is laid upon the principle of unending change, it may end as a revolutionary philosophy. As long as Hegel was alive he was able to hold these contrary tendencies together, but Engels points out that as soon as he died his followers became divided into two camps—a right-wing which upheld the existing order as the manifestation of the absolute, and a left-wing which maintained that this was inconsistent with the dialectical principle.[1] As was only natural, the Right-Hegelians were more acceptable to the authorities than the Left, and after the expulsion of Bruno Bauer from Berlin University, the latter went into political opposition. None the less, they remained idealists. They continued to regard ideas as the moving force in history, and to hold that any revolution must start with a revolution in ideas. With the material conditions of society they were unconcerned.

Now it is important to note that although Marx was extremely hostile to the Left-Hegelians, it is from his criticism of the conservative side of Hegel's philosophy that his doctrine of historical materialism initially derives. Hegel had represented society as the product of the state and the complete embodiment of its will, whereas in the

---

[1] *Feuerbach*, S.W., II, pp. 331–332.

period when he was editing the *Neue Rheinische Zeitung*, Marx had already formed the opinion that it represented the will of the governing minority only—the germ of his later thesis that all states are instruments of oppression in the hands of a dominant class. He therefore inverted Hegel's teaching. The state is the product of society, and the Hegelian state is to be rejected as an abstraction unrelated to the real, material life of its citizens. In the ideal state, in which there will be true democracy, there would be no such contradictions as at present exist between the will of the state and that of its citizens. Hegel indeed maintained that this ideal had been achieved in the Prussian state, from which he claimed that all contradiction had been removed; and, as MacIntyre observes, this is a fair example of the idealist trend of his philosophy, in which a conceptual system is substituted for the material reality of nature and history.[1] Marx refused to accept Hegel's conclusion, on the grounds that the Prussian state, with its repressive censorship and omnipotent police, was clearly no ideal state.

Again, Hegel had taught that man had been led to "objectify" the products of his own thought and of the world he had himself created, so that they appeared as external to himself, and that he had thus become "alienated" or estranged from his true nature. This alienation was resolved by man "coming to himself", a process which had also been achieved in the Prussian state, in which alienation had therefore ceased. Marx disputed this, and for the same reason—that it simply was not true.[2]

How, then, was this contradiction between the Hegelian ideal and reality to be overcome? In his search for an answer, Marx was influenced by the French socialist thinkers, and particularly by Saint-Simon, whose writings

[1] A. C. MacIntyre, *Marxism. An Interpretation*, 1953, p. 27.
[2] *op. cit.*, pp. 38 f., 50 f.

had circulated widely in Germany; and from them—and there must also be added the Swiss economist Sismondi— he borrowed, though commonly without acknowledgement, what were to be the specifically sociological features of his future system. But although they directed him to the evils of the existing social order, and gave him valuable insights into its working, they had failed, in his opinion, to discern any central unifying principle behind the phenomena they investigated, and could thus provide no satisfactory explanation as to how that renovation of society, which they all agreed to be necessary, was to be effected. It was for this reason that he was later to describe them as "Utopians", though the charge of utopianism can very well be brought against his own brand of socialism, for all its scientific pretensions.

It was while Marx was still concerned with the contradictions in Hegel's system that he came under the influence of Ludwig Feuerbach. Both he and Engels treated him ungenerously, and were far more concerned to point out where they differed from him than to admit their indebtedness, which was very great. But in his *Feuerbach* (1888) Engels made some tardy amends. He declared that in his *Essence of Christianity* (1841) Feuerbach had "without circumlocution placed materialism on the throne again", and recalled the enthusiasm with which his writings had been greeted—"We all became Feuerbachians".[1] Indeed, in his *National Economy and Philosophy* (1844) Marx says of them that they alone are worthy to stand beside Hegel's *Phenomenology of Spirit* as containing a real theoretical revolution. And goes further. "There is", he says, "no way to truth and freedom save through Feuerbach"—"the bath of fire which is the purgatory through which the present age must pass". Yet although Feuerbach often used language which might suggest the contrary, he did not accept a materialist conception of the

[1] S.W., II, pp. 332–333.

world; for, as he put it, "materialism is for me the *basis* of the edifice, but it is not the edifice itself".[1] What he sought to do was to make man the standard of all values, and to demonstrate, in opposition to Hegel, that every form of human consciousness was materially conditioned. Therein lay what Marx was to describe as his "true humanism".

Thus it was from Feuerbach that Marx got the seminal idea that all the manifestations of the spirit of man have their roots in his material needs, and that history is the attempt of humanity to satisfy these needs, which create an opposition between that which is and that which ought to be. In religion, the most characteristic of these manifestations, man projects his needs into a supernatural order. But in so doing he becomes alienated from himself, because he is transferring to a Supreme Being qualities which belong to his own nature, and which will one day find their true expression in a religion of humanity, when men will become conscious that "the only God of man is man himself". Marx was little interested in this consummation. But he endorsed Feuerbach's attack upon religion, though he revised its premises. The world of religion is an inverted world because it reflects a society which is upside down. Thus it becomes for Marx the starting point of all criticism of society. As he declares in his *Critique of Hegel's Philosophy of Law* (1843–44), "The criticism of heaven transposes itself into a criticism of the earth; the criticism of religion into a criticism of the law; the criticism of theology into a criticism of politics".

What Marx did therefore was to extend Feuerbach's principles to society, or rather to the conditions under which man lives as a member of it: and as these conditions appeared to him to depend primarily upon economic factors, it was into economic terms that he transposed the concept of alienation. In his *National Economy*

[1] Engels, *Feuerbach*, S.W., II, 337.

and Philosophy, in which he is still concerned with the estrangement and ultimate redemption of humanity, he contends that man has become alienated as a result of the institution of private property until, under capitalist production, he is not only the slave of the commodities he makes, but is himself also a commodity, something which is bought and sold in the market, so that he is estranged both from himself and from his fellow men. From this alienation, of which religion is simply an ideological expression, socialism offers the only prospect of release. Then at last man will attain to self-realisation.

Yet in the *Communist Manifesto* Marx singles out this concept of alienation for contemptuous treatment as an example of the way in which the German school of "True Socialists", which he was attacking, converted concrete phenomena into abstractions;[1] and this is singular because, as Pierre Bigo has pointed out in a recent study, his *Capital* is dominated by it. The purpose of that work was to provide the proof of his doctrine of historical materialism, at least as far as the capitalist stage of development is concerned; and Bigo describes it as "an existential analysis of an historic economic system"—existential because it is not an analysis of abstract and mechanical concepts, but of a human situation. This situation is precisely the alienation of man, of which commodity production, capital, money and the like are symbols. For Marx, therefore, political economy is the recognition of this alienation and of the means by which it will be overcome.[2]

We shall have to consider later how far Marx is justified in holding that men become the victims of alienation under a system of private property, and whether socialism will remove those symptoms of it to which he objects. What we have to observe here is that the problem is a

---

[1] For Marx's criticism of this school see Auguste Cornu, "German Utopianism: 'True' Socialism", *Science and Society*, Winter, 1948, pp. 97 f.
[2] *Marxisme et Humanisme*, Paris, 1953, pp. 34–35.

moral one, and as such lies beyond the field of purely empirical enquiry. Marx professes to base his science of society upon the methods of the natural sciences. But these methods are quantitative and not qualitative, and they do not and cannot lead to value-judgements which such concepts as alienation involve. What distinguishes science from non-science is that science deals with data which can be weighed, measured and the like; whereas non-science deals with data which are not amenable to these methods. Bigo is not alone in maintaining that Marx was primarily a humanist, that his goal was a world in which man would realise his true nature and thus find freedom, and that he sought to construct a society in which that goal would be realised. But while this is doubtless true, it was to lead him into positions which cannot be sustained by the methods he claims to be applying, and which have no place in a materialist system.

Marx soon broke away from Feuerbach, and the measure of his disagreement is revealed in the famous *Eleven Theses*, apparently written in March 1845.[1] They were discovered in a notebook after his death, and were printed by Engels as an appendix to his own *Feuerbach*, which they doubtless inspired him to write. They are the most concise formulation of his philosophy that we possess, though how far they are to be taken as representing the thought of his later years is another question. According to Engels, he had no intention of publishing them.

In the *Theses* Marx deals with the relation between consciousness (thought) and being (the external world) which Engels declares in his *Feuerbach* to be the fundamental problem of philosophy. In the first of them he lays down that "the chief defect of all hitherto existing materialism, that of Feuerbach included, had been that while admitting the material nature of reality, it had conceived of it in the form of object or contemplation and not

[1] S.W., II, pp. 365–367.

as subject", or, as he calls it, "sensuous human activity" which determines its own object instead of being determined by it. For unless reality was conceived as active, there was no accounting for why it should ever change. Hegel had not committed this error, but he had only escaped it by falling into another, that is, by endowing the Idea, conceived as both subject and object, with the properties of spontaneity and self-development. What had, then, to be done was to show that the dynamic quality which Hegel attributed to the Idea operated in the world such as our daily experience revealed it to be.

It was here that Feuerbach had missed the mark. He had shown that religion was an illusion, but had made the "essence of man" the source of the illusion.[1] Marx objects that the essence of man is an abstraction; for indeed as soon as we talk of "essences", we are assuming something which is unchangeable, which the dialectic forbids, so that Feuerbach's system becomes a form of idealism. Marx contends therefore that we can only account for why ideas originate and develop if we regard man as a member of society or, as he puts it, as "the totality of his social relations", that is, of the relations he enters into with other men. But what causes him to form such relations? It is in order to satisfy his needs, of which the most elementary is to provide himself with those things he must have if he is to exist at all. Hence the essence of man, or his "social being", is an activity—the activity that we call production—and it is the form which this takes that determines his relations with his fellows.

When therefore Marx declares that "it is not consciousness that determines being, but it is social being that determines consciousness", he means that the activity of man engaged in production, which is always a social activity, is the primary datum—"the first historic act"—see-

[1] See Eric Voegelin, "The Marxian Revolutionary Idea", *Review of Politics*, 1950, pp. 278 f.

ing that it is thus that man enters into history, and that it is this that determines his consciousness. He thus reverses Descartes's dictum, "Cogito, ergo sum". The very opposite is true. Thought is the product of things. Only, if thought is to give knowledge which is genuine, it cannot be divorced from action. To think is to live. To live is to work. To work is to produce. All that man is derives, therefore, from that central creative activity to which he and all his fellows are committed and which is the condition of their very existence. This is production.

At the same time, Marx teaches that consciousness is also a creative activity, and that it is continually changing that social being from which it springs. Thus he lays down in the Second Thesis that "the question as to whether objective truth can be attributed to human thinking is not a question of theory but a practical question". The contemplative reason cannot indeed furnish it, since it only gives us ideas which do not become knowledge until they have been translated into action. Yet we have an assurance that it is attainable; and this is that we are able, by our actions, to transform the world. In his study of the *Theses* N. Rotenstreich points out that this is not pragmatism. For the essence of pragmatism is that reality is irrational. Hence it cannot be known, and all we can do is to judge actions by their consequences. Marx's theory is the exact opposite. Reality is not irrational, and it is knowable because we have ourselves created it.[1]

Yet one element in this theory is far from clear. We are told that we can be certain that we do obtain objective knowledge of the external world—that is, knowledge of that world which is genuine as opposed to the various illusions we may entertain of its nature—because we are

[1] "Marx's Thesen über Feuerbach", *Archiv für Rechts-und Sozialphilosophie*, 1951, pp. 354–355. For Engel's contribution to the above see *Feuerbach*, S.W., II, p. 336, and his introduction to the 1892 English edition of *Socialism: Utopian and Scientific*, S.W., II, pp. 92–93.

all the time testing the ideas we form by acting upon them, just as the scientist tests his own by experimenting with them in his laboratory; and that in fact these ideas do not become genuine knowledge until they have been so tested. And we are told, further, that the test of the truth of ideas is whether they transform the world. But any idea, if acted upon, may do this, and what we want to know is what particular transformations guarantee the truth of those upon which we have acted. Marx does not tell us this, and if he means that only those ideas which move the world in the direction of communism have passed the test, he is adopting an arbitrary criterion, and one which only communists would accept.

It should be observed, finally, that two elements enter into the above theory—the external world of being (the object), which projects its impressions upon our senses, and mind or consciousness (the subject), which receives these impressions. Each is an activity which is inter-related with the other, so that while consciousness is determined by the external world, that world is what it is by reason of the influence of consciousness upon it. The link between the two is "doing", or "praxis" as Marx calls it, a concept which he also took over from Feuer-bach, but again transposed into economic terms by identi-fying "doing" with the labour of man engaged in produc-tion. Now, the first of these elements is common to Marx and to the eighteenth-century materialists, who had derived it from Locke's sensationalist philosophy, and what was original in the theory was the second, which represents mind as active. The earlier materialists had taught that while the impressions we receive through our senses give us knowledge, our minds do no more than pas-sively register them; whereas Marx holds that they do not give us knowledge, but only stimuli to knowledge which are then completed in action.[1] Yet when Engels and

---

[1] Sidney Hook, *Towards an Understanding of Karl Marx*, 1933, p. 37.

Lenin have to deal with the theory of knowledge, they restrict themselves almost exclusively to the first of these elements, and have little to say about the second, and it has therefore been suggested that they failed to understand Marx's theory.[1] The more probable explanation is, however, that as they were both primarily concerned to defend the materialist basis of the Marxist system, they felt no inclination to assert the active role of mind with its embarrassing implications. In Lenin's philosophy it does not enter into the process of knowing, though in his political writings he fully admits that it is active, at least in the form of revolutionary class consciousness. Indeed, he has to admit it. For if man is to be active in history, it can only be through his ideas, so that these ideas constitute an active historical force. Man must be able to act on the world and change it, since otherwise revolutions would not be forms of human activity, but simply incidents in a mechanical process. What we have therefore to enquire is how far man's freedom to do this is consistent with the doctrine of historical materialism.

[1] McFadden, *op. cit.*, pp. 260 f.

IV

Marxism and Determinism

In his important study of the philosophy of Engels, the Italian Marxist, R. Mondolfo, makes Marx's theory of the relation between consciousness and being the key to an understanding of historical materialism, of which he declares the concept of "praxis" to be the "nerve centre". In the dialectic of that process the objective element of the forces of nature and the subjective element of the will of man stand to one another as thesis and anthesis. Seeing therefore that the will is an integral part of the whole process, Mondolfo contends that historical materialism is not materialist, and that the notion that it is rests on a false analogy between it and philosophical materialism. Nor, for the same reason, can it be described as determinist.[1]

Yet Marx and Engels continually confront us with a paradox between a process which is sometimes shown to be dependent on the development of economic forces, even if an interaction between these forces and others is conceded, and one in which the will appears to be the prime mover. In the *Communist Manifesto* it is the latter which is emphasised in the form of revolutionary class consciousness; but it upon the former that the stress comes increasingly to be laid in their later writings, as it was, for example, in the preface to the *Critique of Political Economy*. In his *Poverty of Philosophy* Marx does indeed attack Proudhon for failing to recognise that economic categories are simply the theoretical expression of human relations, by which he means that such a concept as

---

[1] *Il materialismo storico in Federico Engels*, ed. Florence, 1952, esp. chapters X and XII.

"labour" has no significance apart from men and women who work at this or that time and place under such and such conditions; and although he and Engels seem constantly to forget this, it might be argued that, as Engels explains, the reason is that while the subject-matter of political economy is always the relations between persons, and ultimately between classes, these relations take the form of things, and therefore appear as things. But this does not prove the point Mondolfo wants to make, since it is one thing to say that economic categories are reducible to relations between human beings, and another to conclude that the will of these human beings affects the development of society, that is, if that development is as Marx and Engels describe it.

For in his *Capital* Marx goes out of his way to show that that development is altogether independent of human volition. After pointing out in the preface to the first edition that his purpose is to "examine the capitalist mode of production", he explains that this mode is based upon "natural laws", described in the next paragraph as "tendencies working with iron necessity towards inevitable results"; and that once a society has entered upon a given economic system, it must go through with it to the end, and all it can hope to do is to "shorten the birth-pangs" of its transition into a higher order. Thus he concludes, "My standpoint, from which the evolution of the economic formation of society is viewed as a process of natural history, can less than any other make the individual responsible for relationships whose creature he socially is, however much he may subjectively raise himself above them".

Further, in the preface to the second edition he quotes with complacency a review which had appeared in a St. Petersburg journal. "Marx only troubles himself about one thing; to show by rigid scientific investigation the necessity of successive determinate orders of social conditions, and to establish, as impartially as possible, the facts that serve him for fundamental starting points. For this it is quite enough if he proves, at the same time, both the necessity of the present order of things, and the necessity of another order into which the first must inevitably pass over; and this all the same, whether men believe in it or not, whether they are conscious or unconscious of it. Marx treats the social movement as a process of natural history, governed by laws not only independent of human will, but rather, on the contrary, determining that will, consciousness and intelligence."

Again, Marx argues that competition between capitalists compels them to make investments that increase the productivity of labour, and that in so doing they render a great service to mankind. Yet this service is not only rendered without any intention on their part, but is one which runs counter to their own interests, because any increase in the proportion of "constant capital" (e.g. machinery) to "variable" or "wage capital" must result in a decline in the rate of profits.[1] We are not concerned with whether this thesis, which was to lead to so much controversy, is true or not, but simply to point out that here again Marx is recording a process which operates inevitably, and which cannot be ascribed to the "will" of the capitalist, since he is alleged to be ultimately the loser by it.[1] Hence, despite his abuse of exploitation, he never represented capitalists as a class or as individuals as having established themselves by an act of will. They are always, as H. J. Blackham says, "necessary agents of a necessary system", and that they are displaced in due course by new men is not primarily because they are oppressive, but because they are inefficient.[2]

In thus drawing attention to the unforeseen consequences of human action, Marx was making a contribution of real value. Yet it was one which he was only able

[1] K. R. Popper, *The Open Society and its Enemies*, 1945, II, pp. 171–172.
[2] *The Human Tradition*, 1953, p. 103.

to make by playing down the element of will, though he certainly did not want to exclude it because a doctrine of social development which represented men as automata was little calculated to further the cause of revolution. Yet how can the will enter into his scheme? Certainly not as that of individuals, since he does not recognise the individual save as a member of his class, whose interests and opinions he shares, so that its will constitutes a "class will". Nor, even here, can it enter as conscious will. We have seen at what pains Marx is to point out that men are entirely unaware of the forces that are making history. Engels is equally emphatic. In his *Feuerbach* he explains that "the conflict of innumerable individual wills and individual actions in the domain of history produces a state of affairs entirely analogous to that prevailing in the realm of unconscious nature", in which "nothing ever happens as the result of consciously desired aims". "The ends of the actions", he goes on to say, "are intended, but the results which actually follow from these actions are not intended; or when they seem to correspond to the end intended they ultimately have consequences quite other than those intended".[1] Yet behind this conflict of wills and interests there are "the general laws of history" which overrule them and bring order out of chaos. As he points out in one of his letters, "the historical event" to which the conflict of wills gives rise "may be viewed as the product of a process which, taken as a whole, works unconsciously and without volition", seeing that "what each individual wants is obstructed by everyone else, and what emerges is something that no one willed". Yet he assures his correspondent that this does not mean that the individual wills are of no value, since they have all contributed to the ultimate "resultant". How they have done so he does not explain.[2] His doctrine is indeed not far removed from that of the har-

[1] S.W., II, p. 354.　[2] To Joseph Bloch, Sept. 21, 1890, *Corresp.*, p. 476.

mony of interests, according to which men in pursuit of their own ends bring about a common good which they had never intended, a view which had influenced Hegel through Adam Smith as suggesting a purpose in history behind that of the individual.

In his *Anti-Dühring* Engels declares, however, that the situation becomes transformed when men understand the real forces operating in history, since these forces thereafter cease to resemble those which operate in nature, that is, they no longer work "blindly, violently and destructively". "Once we have recognised them and understand how they work . . . the gradual subjection of them to our wills and the use of them for the attainment of our end depends entirely upon ourselves."[1] Yet he points out in the conclusion of the same section that it is only when society has taken over the means of production that men are released from the forces which have hitherto constrained them, and their social organisation at last becomes their own voluntary act. Then and then only do they acquire that mastery over their destiny which enables them "to leap from the kingdom of necessity into the kingdom of freedom".[2] But to understand the nature of these forces is not enough. There must also be a "social act", that is, men must be prepared to use their knowledge. This indeed implies conscious will. Yet, as Engels is never weary of insisting, the proletariat did not possess the knowledge which generates the act of will until Marx had revealed it.

According to the Soviet economist, A. Leontiev, economic law is the expression of "objective necessity" in any socio-economic structure. But, whereas under capitalism it manifests itself in laws which operate independently of the will and consciousness of man, under socialism it does so as "conscious necessity", that is, as laws whose operation is now determined by the will and consciousness of

[1] p. 313.   [2] p. 318.

society as a whole.[1] Yet Lenin asserts the exact opposite. In his *What "The Friends of the People" Are* he ridicules S. Krivshenko for attributing to Marx the view that if men wanted to, and acted accordingly, they could avoid the vicissitudes of capitalism. His comment upon this is, "? ! ! According to Marx therefore the evolution of social and economic relationships is determined by human will and consciousness. Is this boundless ignorance or unexampled effrontery?"[2] But in the preface to the Russian edition of Marx's *Letters to Kugelmann* he declares that, "*Above all everything else* Marx put the fact that the working class heroically, self-sacrificingly and taking the initiative makes history".[3] In fact he no more desires to exclude the will than do Marx and Engels, but they are all thinking as it were on two independent planes which never meet.

Marxism–Leninism accepts the Hegelian notion that "freedom is the knowledge of necessity". We are bound by laws, but we can either accept them with passive and uncomprehending acquiescence, or seek to understand their nature and turn them to our ends. It is in proportion as we do this last that we attain freedom. Now no one disputes that a system does not become determinist because it is governed by laws. What is disputable is whether society is governed by the laws which Marx imposes on it, whether these laws possess the same validity as the laws of the natural sciences to which they are declared to be analogous, and whether, if these assump-

---

[1] "On the Problems of the Political Economy of Socialism", *Planovoe Khoziaistvo*, No. 6, 1947, quoted by A. Zauberman, "Economic Thought in the Soviet Union", *Review of Economic Studies*, 1948–1949, p. 3.

[2] S.W., I, p. 418.

[3] Quoted by V. Adoratsky, *Dialectical Materialism*, 1934, p. 87. None the less, Lenin always insisted that the policy of the Bolsheviks and the revolution they carried out was strictly determined by the "objective conditions" of the time. As he puts it, the party chooses "the path prescribed by the objective progress of events", though it alone has that insight into the laws of history which enables it to discern what that path is (see N. Leites, *A Study of Bolshevism*, 1954, pp. 75–77).

tions be accepted, that freedom which has been identified with the recognition of necessity is consistent with man's freedom of choice. What is his relation to society? Is he determined by its social structure, or is he merely conditioned by it? It is an issue of the first importance. Yet here again we are baffled by Marx's disinclination to define his terms, since he uses *bedingt* (determines) and *bestimmt* (conditions) as though they both meant the same. If, however, man is determined by the form society takes, we can hardly say that he is free; while if he is only conditioned by it, we cannot speak of "economic determinism". In fact Marxist–Leninist theory seeks to make the best of both worlds, by representing society as determined by economic forces, but man as only conditioned by them.[1]

But now let us look into this Hegelian formula a little more closely. It sounds reasonable enough. The airman is free in so far as he understands the laws of flying and identifies himself with them. He will recognise them as a part of the order of nature, and will not suppose that they can be other than they are. Similarly, Hegel and Marx tell us that the individual is free who regards history as a process which develops according to a rational pattern, and understands the necessities that govern the process and so make the pattern what it is. Such a man will not seek to oppose to the march of history his private opinions, approving this part of it and condemning that, for this would not be to act as a rational being. Yet where does this in practice lead us? To the suppression of the individual altogether. His right to pass judgement is taken from him, save in so far as it is merely the acceptance of what is because it must be, and he himself becomes an unconsidered fragment. In Hegel's scheme, he is only a fully "real" being as a member of the state, and in Marx's as a member of society engaged in material production.

[1] McFadden, *op. cit.*, pp. 229 f.

Both systems are equally determinist. The individual as such does not count. All that matters is the pattern.

Now, it would be unfair to blame Marx for having failed to solve a problem which is insoluble, but with which our human situation continually confronts us. We live in a world that is governed by laws, and at the same time we believe, or at least the majority of us do so, that within their framework we possess freedom of choice. But precisely how far these laws restrict our freedom, or how far our freedom enables us to modify their operation, we cannot tell, nor can we expect Marx to do so. None the less, we are justified in saying that the dialectic inevitably led him to tilt the scales towards the element of restraint and away from that of freedom, so that his doctrine of historical materialism came to assume a strictly determinist form, which it need not otherwise have done. Every system of production is shown to have broken down on account of its inherent contradictions—contradictions which had to arise and for which the next inevitable stage in the dialectical process provided the only solution. How the will can influence such a process is hard to see. We are told, indeed, that capitalist production, by intensifying social injustice, brings into existence its "grave-diggers" in the form of the proletariat, who will end by organising themselves to destroy it; and it is on account of this "act of will" that it is contended that historical materialism is not materialist. But even assuming that the proletariat will behave in this manner, which Lenin held that it would never do if left to itself, its revolution is simply an inevitable reflex action which takes place when production reaches a certain level of development, and is determined by it.

An American Marxist has stated that, "Marx regards events in history as consequences of the desires and wishes of human beings. According to this theory it is evident that society can guide and determine its destiny.

History acts according to certain laws. The merit of Marx consists in the discovery of these laws."[1] But this is pure assertion, seeing that the relation between the "desires and wishes of human beings" and the laws in accordance with which history acts is left undetermined. Admittedly revolutions are carried out by persons or groups of persons, and if no one is willing to undertake them, they will not take place. Yet, according to the Marxist thesis, they cannot occur at all until the requisite economic pre-conditions have been satisfied, and whether or not they have been is independent of the will of man. It may well be, as Mondolfo argues, that this is inconsistent with Marx's doctrine of the relation between consciousness and being as set out in the *Theses on Feuerbach*;[2] but the activity of mind upon which he insists so strongly in that doctrine is after all an idealist concept which has no place in a system which is then represented as materialist.

What Marx set out to do was to construct a doctrine of social development which would be strictly scientific because it would be based on empirical data, and would thus exclude such concepts as "eternal justice" to which the "Utopian Socialists" had appealed. He had therefore to demonstrate that changes within society take place in accordance with laws which operate inexorably and independently of the will of man. At the same time, his writings and those of Engels contain many passages which imply that the will of man is the decisive factor, as it has to be if the appeal "Workers of the world unite" is to be more than rhetoric. But what we want to know is how it does enter into history as an active force, and the answer to this is not at all clear. For sometimes, as G. D. H. Cole points out, economic forces are endowed with a will which is independent of the will of man, sometimes the will of man is treated as a part of these forces, while sometimes it

---

[1] A. S. Sachs, *Basic Principles of Socialism*, New York, 1925, pp. 105–106.
[2] pp. 249 f.

is represented as something upon which these forces operate from without.[1] Marx tells us that "men make their
own history, but they do not make it under conditions
chosen by themselves".[2] But, while he shows how true is
the second part of this statement, he is not by any means
as successful in establishing the truth of the first. Indeed,
as the American Marxist, Vernon Venable, says, he would
have had to admit that in so far as men do make history,
they have so far made it very badly.[3]

[1] *Socialist Thought. The Forerunners* (1789–1850), 1953, p. 173.
[2] *Eighteenth Brumaire*, S.W., I, p. 222.
[3] *Human Nature—The Marxian View*, 1946, p. 78.

V

Production

With the *Theses on Feuerbach* Marx took leave of philosophy. Hegel had solved the problem of development as far as philosophy could do so—by translating concrete phenomena into abstract categories and then showing how they passed dialectically from one into another, and as there was nothing more for it to do, he had brought it to an end. Marx converts Hegel's categories into economic forces, and makes these the basis of reality. This reality man creates by acting upon it, and the way he does so is through the social activity of production; thus history becomes a record of changes in production, or economic history.

How, then, does the dialectic enter into this process? As we have seen, it is the belief that development takes place as a result of conflict, that this conflict must be one between two forces and two forces only, and that it must end in a synthesis on a higher level. To be able to use the dialectic, Marx had therefore to show that production gives rise to such a conflict of forces and explain what they were. His thesis is therefore that every system of production has given rise to "contradictions" or "antagonistic forces" (he does not distinguish between the two) which have led to its destruction and to the emergence of a new and more highly developed system. They are reflected in the division of society into classes, but the class struggle allegedly resulting from this is a matter which calls for separate treatment, and we need only note here that it was the development of production which was originally responsible for bringing classes into existence at all, and has since determined the form they have taken. The capitalist system, like its predecessors, has developed its own peculiar antagonisms or contradictions, which will eventually lead to its replacement first by socialism and then by communism, when at last production will be carried out in such a way as no longer to give rise to them. Hence it is they which provide the element of conflict that the dialectic requires.

Marx first defines his position as a sociologist in his *National Economy and Philosophy*, in which appear the major theses that he was to develop in his later writings. From Hegel's *Phenomenology of Spirit* he borrows the conception of the progressive evolution of man through labour, though he complains that the only labour Hegel knew was spiritual labour, and gives it a wider extension by making it cover human activity in general, so that, as he puts it, "All forms of human activity, whether mental or physical, are simply particular forms of production and fall under its general laws". Thus he concludes, "The whole of the so-called history of the world is nothing but the production of man by human labour".[1]

In the *National Economy and Philosophy*, however, Marx's thought is still revolving round the problem of alienation, the basic form of which is now shown to be due to the perverted relations in which men stand to production under private enterprise. But in the *German Ideology*, written in collaboration with Engels in 1845–46, though unpublished in their lifetime, this discovery leads to a quite different approach—to the attempt to construct a theory of society which "can be verified in a purely empirical way". As MacIntyre says, prophecy is henceforth abandoned for prediction. "Communism is no longer something which ought to be, but something which must be."[2]

Thus it is in the *German Ideology* that we find the first of the many statements Marx and Engels were to make as to

[1] Marx–Engels Gesamtausgabe = M.E.G.A., Abt. I, Bd. 3, p. 135.
[2] *op. cit.*, p. 69.

what historical materialism is. "We must begin by stating the first premise of human existence and therefore of all history, that man must be in a position to live in order to 'make his history'. But life involves before anything else eating and drinking, a habitation and many other things. The first historical act is thus the production of the means to satisfy these needs, the production of material life itself. . . . The first necessity in any theory of history is to observe this fundamental fact in all its significance, and accord to it due importance".[1]

Marx then explains that production depends on "the nature of the means of subsistence", which constitute what he calls the "productive forces", and by these he apparently means the natural resources of which men dispose at any given time. But he then points out that production is not simply a physical activity. It is also a way of life, seeing that "what men are is determined both by *what* they produce and the *way* they produce it". For the "productive forces" (still undefined) lead men to enter into a relationship with one another which is determined by the nature of these forces. This relationship he calls the "social relations", a term for which he later substituted the "relations of production" or "production relations". It is true that in the *German Ideology* he declares that "a certain mode of production or industrial stage is always combined with a certain mode of co-operation, and this mode of co-operation is itself a 'productive force' ", but elsewhere, and especially in the preface to the *Critique of Political Economy*, the most complete statement he ever made of what historical materialism is, the productive forces and the relations of production are treated as independent though inter-related aspects of production, the productive forces being primary, and giving rise to relations of production appropriate to and dependent on them.

[1] M.E.G.A., Abt. I, Bd. 5, p. 16; Eng. trans., ed. R. Pascal, 1938, p. 16.

Considering the importance which Marx attached to production, it is a pity that he does not explain more precisely what he means by it. The nearest he comes to doing so is in *Capital* where "the elementary factors of the labour process" are defined as "(*a*) the personal activity of man—*i.e.*, the work itself; (*b*) the subject of that work, and (*c*) its instruments".[1] The instruments, he points out, are an extension of human activity, "something which man annexes to his own body, adding stature to himself in spite of the Bible".[2] "The subject of the work" are "the means of subsistence ready to hand, subjects spontaneously provided by nature". "The personal activity of man" is presumably introduced because raw materials and tools have no significance apart from the men who develop the one with the aid of the other. Venable, following Marx, interprets it as "purposive human activity", and this may stand if it means no more than that men possess certain aptitudes and apply them with a knowledge of what they are doing.[3]

As for the "relations of production", nowhere is any attempt made to define them. In effect, they denote the various phenomena to which the development of any given complex of productive forces gives rise, and in the preface to the *Critique of Political Economy* Marx says that their sum total constitutes "the economic structure of society".[4] Under feudalism they include the guilds and corporations;[5] and under "bourgeois production", credit

---

[1] Moore and Aveling's translation of the third German edition, ed. 1946, I, pp. 157–158.
[2] See R. Ruyer, "Marx et Butler ou Technologie et Finalisme", *Revue de la Métaphysique et de la Morale*, 1950, pp. 302 f.   [3] *op. cit.*, p. 88.
[4] S.W., I, p. 329; but cp. Engel's letter to Heinz Starkenburg of Jan. 25, 1894 (*Corresp.*, p. 516) in which "the methods by which human beings in a given society produce their means of subsistence and exchange the products among themselves", which he calls the "economic conditions", are made to include the "entire technique of production and transport" which the *Communist Manifesto* had specifically assigned to the productive forces (S.W., I, p. 37).
[5] Letter to P. V. Annenkov, Dec. 28, 1846, *Corresp.*, p. 8.

and money.[1] In his *Wage Labour and Capital*, capital is described as a "bourgeois production relation",[2] and this is consistent with the definition of it in *Capital* as "dead labour", that is, labour which has been bought and paid for, and has thus ceased to be a productive force.[3] In the preface to the *Critique*, and indeed in the *Communist Manifesto* also, the relations of production are virtually identified with the property system which is declared to be "but the legal expression of the same thing". John Plamenatz argues that if the property system is the "legal expression" of the relations, it cannot be the relations themselves.[4] But while Marx is not at all clear, what he appears to mean is that the characteristic form which property assumes, and of which the property system is the "legal expression", depends upon the degree of development of the productive forces, so that under an agricultural economy it will be land, and under a capitalist economy, the ownership of a business or shares in it. In this sense, property can be represented as, broadly speaking, a "relation of production", and indeed as the most important of such relations, since it is the one with which the dominant class will least desire interference.

In his *Dialectical and Historical Materialism* (1938) Stalin follows Marx, and his treatment has at least the merit of lucidity. On the one hand, there are the instruments of production, the people who use them and their experience and skill, and these collectively constitute the productive forces; while, on the other, there are the relations of production to which these forces give rise, and which are either relations of co-operation or of exploitation or transitional from one form to the other. "Consequently", he

---

[1] *The Poverty of Philosophy*, ed. Chicago, 1910, p. 114.
[2] S.W., I, p. 84.
[3] I, p. 216; cp. Engels; "The so-called 'productivity of capital' is nothing but the quality attached to it (under present-day social relations, without which it would not be capital at all) of being able to appropriate the unpaid labour of wageworkers", *The Housing Question*, S.W., I, p. 518.
[4] *German Marxism and Russian Communism*, 1954, p. 22.

says, "production, or the mode of production, embraces both the productive forces of society and men's relations of production, and is thus the embodiment of their unity in the process of the production of material values." [1] He notes among the characteristics of production that "its changes and development always begin with changes and development of the productive forces, and in the first place with changes and development of the instruments of production". The Soviet *Political Dictionary* of 1940 obediently echoed the above by declaring the productive forces to be "the most mobile, revolutionary and also determining element in the development of production", and this was repeated in almost the same words in the edition of the *Short Philosophic Dictionary* of 1952.

Venable argues that the above analysis establishes no case for identifying the development of production with that of technology, as has been done by certain Marxists, and in particular by Labriola.[2] Yet Stalin represents the two as virtually identical, and both the *Political* and the *Philosophic Dictionaries* hold changes in production to be "primarily changes in the instruments of production". To this view both Marx and Engels lend authority. The preface to the *Critique of Political Economy* refers, indeed, only to the development of the productive forces and does not mention technology. Yet, as Marx says in *Capital*, "It is not the articles made, but how they are made, and by what instruments, that enables us to distinguish different economic epochs".[3] And again: "Technology discloses man's mode of dealing with Nature, the process of production by which he sustains his life, and thereby also lays bare the mode of formation of his social relations, and of the mental conceptions that flow from them".[4] Similarly, he points out in *Wage Labour and Capital* that it is the tech-

---

[1] *Leninism*, ed., 1940, p. 67.
[2] *op. cit.*, p. 92; see also M. M. Bober, *Karl Marx's Interpretation of History*, Harvard University Press, ed. 1950, pp. 6–11.
[3] I, p. 159.   [4] *ibid.*, p. 367 n.

nology of production that determines the relations of production, and thus the form that society takes, just as it is the type of weapon used that determines the organisation of an army; [1] and indeed in a letter to Engels of July 7, 1866 he asks whether there is "anywhere where our theory that the *organisation of labour is determined by the means of production* is more brilliantly confirmed" than in the army or, as he prefers to call it, "the human slaughter industry".[2] Engels held the same view. "According to our conception, the technique of production ultimately determines the class division . . . and thus the state, law, politics etc." [3] The reason for this emphasis is obvious. Technology does at least provide the basis of a theory of historical development which loses all its precision if other factors are allowed to enter.

The theory starts, therefore, by declaring that the development of production takes place through a series of epochs or modes of production similar to the geological ages, since each is preceded by some sort of cataclysm. There are five of them—primitive communism, slavery, feudalism, capitalism and communism, the last belonging to the future. Primitive communism and its transition into slavery is analysed at some length by Engels in *The Origin of the Family, Private Property and State* (1884), which was based on the conclusions that he and Marx had reached from their study of the American anthropologist, Lewis H. Morgan's *Ancient Society*.[4] At the stage of what Marx calls "asiatic" and Engels "gentile" society, classes did not exist, and whatever was produced was common property. They originate with "division of labour", which is identified in the *German Ideology* with the institution of

---

[1] S.W., I, p. 83.

[2] *Corresp.*, p. 209.

[3] Letter to Heinz Starkenburg, Jan. 25, 1894, *ibid.*, p. 516.

[4] On Morgan's theories and their influence on Marx and Engels see Ernest Seilliere, "Lewis H. Morgan et la philosophie marxiste de l'histoire", *Revue Germanique*, Jan.–Feb., 1907, pp. 1–20; see also Bernard J. Stern, "Engels and the Family", *Science and Society*, Winter, 1948, pp. 42–64.

private property.[1] In his *Origin of the Family* Engels distinguishes three "great social divisions of labour", of which the first two occurred in the stage which he calls "barbarism". In the first, men learn to domesticate animals, and thus to produce more than they require for their immediate subsistence. The herds originally belonged to the community, but in time they became private property. Engels admits that we do not know the reason for this, and all he has to tell us is that they "drifted into the hands of private individuals". This led to the division of society into masters and slaves. Further, it destroyed the equality which had previously existed between the sexes, since it was the men who owned the herds, and the function of the women was now restricted to household duties, so that, as Engels puts it, "in the family the husband is the bourgeois and the wife represents the proletariat." [2]

The next great division takes place in the higher stage of barbarism when "iron becomes the servant of man". Handicrafts now become separated from agriculture, giving rise to production for exchange rather than for use, and to an increased demand for labour. We are now in the second epoch of which slavery, hitherto nascent, is the basis. This brings us to the threshold of civilisation, inaugurated by an extension of division of labour which intensifies that specialisation which Marx and Engels agree in regarding as its most objectionable feature. The Middle Ages, the third epoch of feudalism, creates "a third division of labour peculiar to itself and of decisive importance"—that between industry and commerce. Engels calls those connected with the latter "a class of parasites" who render "very insignificant services", though if this be so, it is not clear why they should have arisen or why the fact that they did so should be regarded as important. The continual expansion of production and

[1] M.E.G.A., Abt. I, Bd. 5, p. 39; Eng. trans., p. 44.
[2] S.W., I, pp. 211-212.

exchange leads in due course to the breakdown of the mediaeval guild system, and to the passage from feudalism into capitalism, first in the form of manufacture, under which the workers, though now crowded into factories, at least make some part of the commodity with their own hands; and then into machinofacture, when they become the slaves of the machine and no longer make anything themselves. And as little skill is required for such work, they become the easier to replace, so that their wages are forced down to the subsistence level, and they are obliged to drive their wives and children to work under the same inhuman conditions as themselves. That is, if they can get work; for the capitalist will use his profits to install labour-saving machinery, which will enable him as far as possible to dispense with their services. Thus, under capitalist production, the proletarian workers become increasingly degraded, though how in this event they are to develop those qualities which will enable them to take over production from the bourgeoisie is one of the unexplained mysteries of the Marxist system.

It is of interest to note, however, that in his *Anti-Dühring* Engels gives a somewhat different account of the stages through which division of labour has passed. "The first great division of labour" (he does not tell us whether there were any others) is the separation of town and country, which establishes a gulf between agriculture and industry, and which the *Origin of the Family* represents as the "second great division", and assigns to the higher stage of barbarism.[1] But the *German Ideology* had laid down that division of labour becomes "truly such" (*wirklich*) only when mental labour is divorced from physical labour;[2] and that "the greatest division" of the two was the separation of town and country, which is stated to have begun with the transition from barbarism into

[1] pp. 324, 326.
[2] M.E.G.A., Abt. I, Bd. 5, p. 21; Eng. trans., p. 20.

civilisation, and indeed can scarcely have taken place in any intelligible sense at an earlier stage.[1] In this event the first "great division of labour" to which Engels refers in the *Origin of the Family* would not appear to have been a genuine division.

The second part of the theory purports to explain that the stages through which society has passed were not accidental, as they were rendered necessary by the development of the productive forces. It might be asked why society should wish to see them developed if the consequences are to be so calamitous. But it is essential to the Marxist thesis that society has no voice in the matter. The development of the productive forces is an inevitable process, and one which in the long run nothing can arrest. A people may be unable to exploit those at its disposal, but in this event it is only a matter of time before its place is taken by another which will do so. Similarly, custom and tradition may hold up their development for centuries, but they cannot do so indefinitely, as this would be to oppose the march of history.

That the productive forces have to be developed, and that this is the cause of exploitation, was a central issue in Engels' famous controversy with Dühring. For Dühring had argued that "the formation of *political* relationships is *historically the fundamental fact*, and the economic conditions dependent on this are consequently always *facts of the second* order". The varying forms in which men have been exploited throughout history, as for example Robinson Crusoe's exploitation of Friday, were thus due to an original act of force which was political and not economic. But Engels contends that Crusoe could never have exploited Friday had not the productive forces at his disposal been developed to the point at which it became possible for him to do so.[2] Historically, private property—

---

[1] M.E.G.A., Abt. I, Bd. 5, p. 39; Eng. trans., p. 43.
[2] *Anti-Dühring*, pp. 181 f.

the basis of exploitation—is not the result of force [1]
(though Marx was always prepared to say that it was so
when it suited his purpose), but "of altered conditions of
production and exchange in the interests of increased production . . . that is to say, as a result of economic causes".[2]
Engels goes on to point out that "the mere fact that the
ruled and exploited class has at all times been more numerous than the rulers and exploiters, and that it is therefore the former that have had the real force in their hands,
is enough to demonstrate the absurdity of the whole force
theory".[3]

This scarcely provides an explanation of why throughout recorded history a minority has been able to victimise
the majority, especially if it is admitted that the latter has
always been the stronger of the two. Engels, however, is
not really concerned with this problem, but rather to show
that exploitation cannot arise at all until the productive
forces have reached a certain level, and that it is upon
these forces that depends the form it has thereafter taken.
Under primitive communism they are socially owned, but
they are scarcely developed at all, and so bitter is the
struggle for existence that the stranger who is caught tres-
passing on the territory of the family or tribe is killed at
once, as there is no means of supporting him.[4] With their
gradual development we pass into the stage of slavery,
which Engels calls "a great step forward", when it becomes possible to keep your captive alive and make him
work for you, in which condition, however miserable, he
does at least enjoy more freedom than if he were dead.[5]
As the productive forces develop still further, slavery is
replaced by feudalism, under which the serf is bound to
his lord's land but his person is respected, as that of the
slave was not. Then they take another leap forward and

---

[1] *Anti-Dühring*, p. 146.   [2] *ibid.*, p. 184.
[3] *ibid.*, p. 203.   [4] *The Origin of the Family*, S.W., II, pp. 195–196.
[5] *Anti-Dühring*, pp. 206–207.

we enter the present stage of capitalism. Here also the worker is exploited, but he possesses greater freedom than did the mediaeval serf. Thus the freedom of man has advanced *pari passu* with the development of the productive forces, in accordance with the view which both Hegel and Marx accepted that history is the record of its progressive realisation.

Each of the above stages has brought into existence a dominant class which has owed its power to the fact that it was the best fitted at the time to develop the existing productive forces. Yet sooner or later it has entrenched itself behind the relations of production to which these forces have given rise, and it has then ceased to be progressive and has become reactionary. Hence every major change in production is always the work of a new class, and is carried out in the teeth of opposition from the class whose interest it is to maintain the existing order. The resistance put up a little more than a century ago by the landed aristocracy to the development of railways by the rising bourgeoisie is a case in point. The bourgeoisie, which was responsible for introducing the capitalist system, was in its day the most progressive element in society. But Marx and Engels contend that it is no longer able to develop the productive forces and is acting as a fetter upon them. It has carried out its mission, and the class predestined to take its place is the proletariat. Then will be fulfilled the last act in the great drama of the emancipation of man, and there will be established a kingdom of justice in which for the first time the productive energies of men will be liberated from exploitation and will be directed to the common good.

While therefore Marx and Engels make no secret of their desire to see the capitalist system abolished, they do not condemn it, nor can they do so without destroying their case.[1] In fact they pay glowing tributes to its achieve-

[1] Cp. Engels' review of *Capital* (March, 1868), S.W., I, p. 425.

ments, and deal severely with such writers as Proudhon and Sismondi, whose aversion to it had led them to advocate a return to a more primitive economy.[1] It is representated as an inevitable stage in the dialectic of production. Yet, like every other mode of production, it has developed contradictions which must ultimately lead to its collapse. Of these the most glaring is that between what Engels calls "social production and private appropriation". For while production is becoming increasingly a social function—something which the individual can do only in co-operation with others—the product does not belong to the men who produce it but to the owners of capital.

Lenin's *Imperialism: The Highest Stage of Capitalism* is held by the faithful to be an important extension of the above, and it may indeed claim to be the most revolutionary writing of the present century, seeing that the strategy of the world communist movement has been largely based on its conclusions. What in fact he was attempting was to explain why, contrary to Marx's predictions, capitalism had not collapsed; and this he did by introducing imperialism as a new factor which Marx could not take into account, as it had not come into existence in his day. Capital, he argued, had changed from industrial into finance capital, and was now primarily employed to develop backward areas to which the metropolitan countries could sell, in exchange for cheap raw materials, the products which their own home markets could not absorb. The profits thus obtained enabled the capitalists to stave off revolution by bribing their own proletariat with higher wages and cheap food at the expense of the native proletariat of the countries they exploited. He went on to insist that imperialism had led

---

[1] On Proudhon see *The Housing Question*, S.W., I, p. 513, and on Sismondi, *The Poverty of Philosophy*, p. 73, and the *Communist Manifesto*, S.W., I, p. 54; cp. D. Riazanov, *The Communist Manifesto*, New York, 1928, pp. 210, 223 f.

to a further series of contradictions within the capitalist system which heralded its final disintegration. As summarised by Stalin in *Foundations of Leninism*, these were (*a*) the original contradiction between capital and labour, (*b*) that between the imperialist powers which were rivals for the control of exploitable territories, and (*c*) that between those powers and the peoples they exploited.[1] According to Marxist–Leninist theory, these contradictions were the cause of the two World Wars, and were intensified by each of them, thus developing a world revolutionary situation such as did not exist in Marx's day.

Every mode of production has thus ended by breaking down on account of its internal contradictions, and both Marx and Lenin represent the capitalist system as being in its death-agony. As we have seen, the productive forces of each mode give rise to relations of production which are at first appropriate to them, and in his *Economic Problems of Socialism in the U.S.S.R.* (1952) Stalin raised the correspondence between the two to the dignity of an economic law.[2] But in the preface to the *Critique of Political Economy* Marx explains that eventually a conflict arises which destroys the correspondence that had previously existed between them, and that it is above all with the property system of the relations that it occurs. "From forms of development of the productive forces these relations change into their fetters. Then begins the epoch of social revolution."[3] Here he is merely stating somewhat more precisely the position he had adopted in his earlier writings. In the *German Ideology* he had declared that "all the collisions of history have their origin in contradictions between the productive forces and the relations of production".[4] Similarly, in his letter to P. V. Annenkov of December 1846 he had said that "when new productive

[1] *Leninism*, ed. 1940, pp. 3–4.   [2] p. 55.   [3] S.W., I, p. 329.
[4] M.E.G.A., Abt. I, Bd. 5, p. 63; Eng. trans., p. 73.

forces are won, men change their method of production, and with the method of production all the economic relations".[1] So also, "In acquiring fresh productive forces, men change their mode of production—the way of getting their livelihood—they change all their social relations. The handmill gives you feudal society; the steam-mill society with the industrial capitalist".[2] And again, "The social relations within which individuals produce, the social relations of production, are altered, transformed, with the change and development of the material means of production, the forces of production." [3]

Engels follows Marx. It is true that in one passage in his *Feuerbach* he so far forgets himself as to include among the productive forces "division of labour and the combination of many workers, each producing a particular part in one complete manufacture", whereas this clearly belongs to the relations of production; but when he proceeds in the same paragraph to describe the origin of the capitalist system, he explains that the new productive forces represented by the bourgeoisie became incompatible with the order of production represented by the feudal landlords and guild masters.[4] It will be observed therefore that both here and in the passages cited from Marx's writings changes in production are represented as initiated by changes in the productive forces which lead to a conflict with the relations of production. They imply a change in the technology of production, since the expression "new productive forces" has no meaning if these forces do not represent an advance upon those they have superseded.

Marx points out, however, that the conflict does not reach the revolutionary stage until the existing productive forces have been developed to their fullest extent.

[1] *Corresp.*, p. 8.
[2] *The Poverty of Philosophy*, Éditions Sociales, 1946, p. 88.
[3] *Wage Labour and Capital*, S.W., I, p. 83.
[4] S.W., II, p. 357.

"No social order ever perishes before all the productive forces for which there is room in it have developed; and new, higher relations of production never appear before the particular conditions for their existence have matured within the womb of the old society itself".[1] Yet he offers no criterion for determining when these conditions have been satisfied, as they certainly had not been when the *Communist Manifesto* appeared; nor even when Engels asserted in his *Anti-Dühring*, written nearly forty years later, that the capitalist system had no further contribution to make, whereas, as Charles Rist observes, X-rays, the internal-combustion engine, aviation and synthetic chemistry, all of which were developed under private enterprise, did not yet exist.[2]

Indeed it would be of interest to know when the golden age of capitalism took place during which it accomplished the wonders with which the *Communist Manifesto* duly credits it, and when, according to Stalin, the productive forces and the relations of production were in correspondence.[3] It cannot have been before the third quarter of the eighteenth century, since it was not until then that, after passing through the quantitative changes of manufacture, it became capitalism proper with the qualitative leap into machinofacture. Yet the *Manifesto* declares that, "For many a decade past, the history of industry and commerce is but the history of the revolt of the modern productive forces against modern conditions of production, against the property relations which are the conditions for the existence of the bourgeoisie and its rule".[4] But this is directly contrary to what Marx had told Annenkov a year earlier; "Up to the year 1825—the period of the first general crisis—the general demand of consumption increased more rapidly than production, and

[1] Preface to *The Critique of Political Economy*, S.W., I, p. 329.
[2] "Marx Utopiste", *Revue d'Economie Politique*, Jan.–Feb., 1948, p. 31.
[3] *Economic Problems of Socialism in the USSR*, p. 57.
[4] S.W., I, 38.

the development of machinery was a necessary consequence of the needs of the market. Since 1825, the invention and application of machinery has been simply the result of war between workers and employers." [1] According to Engels, large-scale industry dates from 1815, while it was not until 1830 that the productive forces of capitalism had developed to the point at which the proletariat first emerged as an element in the class struggle.[2] All therefore we can conclude from the above is that these forces had been fully developed before the capitalist system can properly be said to have existed at all.

Marxist–Leninists, however, use Marx's statement to explain that the capitalist system could not have arisen in the Middle Ages, as the productive forces of feudalism had not yet worked themselves out; and that it would have been still less possible for it to have done so under a pre-feudal mode of production, as this would have meant jumping an entire stage in the dialectical process. But this last was impermissible, as Marx had declared in the preface to the first volume of *Capital* that, "even when a society has got upon the right track for the discovery of the natural laws of its movement . . . it can neither clear by bold leaps nor remove by legal enactments the obstacles offered by the successive stages of its normal development", and by this he had been understood to mean that production must pass through certain prescribed historical phases, of which capitalism was one. As we shall see, this conclusion was to cause him embarrassment when he was required to give a ruling as to whether Russia could achieve socialism upon the basis of the peasant commune, thus by-passing the capitalist stage; and the Mensheviks, as orthodox Marxists, were later to attribute the shortcomings of the Bolshevik Revolution to the fact that it had not been built upon the foundations of a

---

[1] Letter of December 28, 1846, *Corresp.*, p. 10; cp. *The Poverty of Philosophy*, p. 111.　　　　[2] *Feuerbach*, S.W., II, p. 356.

genuine bourgeois-democratic revolution, that is, one which had developed within a capitalist economy. But it was only at the end of his life that Marx was confronted with this Russian problem, and by this time he had already formulated his analysis of the modes of production, and had laid down that a major change could only occur when the productive forces of a given mode had reached their maximum development, and that it would begin with the emergence of new productive forces, to the development of which the existing relations of production had become an obstacle.

Now this sequence provides a reasonably accurate description of the transition from feudalism into capitalism—the subject in which Marx was primarily interested—as the change from manufacture into machinofacture was undoubtedly due to the emergence of new productive forces which led to corresponding changes in the relations of production. His error lay in concluding that it was a universal law which could be used to explain the origin of any mode of production, though he had not studied the pre-capitalist modes with sufficient attention to be able to furnish any proof of this. Thus no attempt is made to show what changes in production led to the replacement of slavery by feudalism—an essentially agricultural economy in which the peasant cultivated the land in much the same way as the slave had done. Again, Marx dates capitalism in the form of manufacture from the middle of the sixteenth century, and represents it as a change in the status of the organisation of labour only. There was no change in the productive forces until the transition into machinofacture, which did not take place for over two centuries. "At first", he says, "capitalism subordinates labour on the basis of the technical conditions in which it historically finds it. It does not therefore change immediately the mode of production." [1] What therefore

[1] *Capital*, I, p. 297.

differentiated early capitalism from feudalism was a change in the status of the worker, that is, in the relations of production, a view which is opposed to that expressed elsewhere that, as these relations merely reflect the productive forces, they cannot change until the latter have done so, any more than a man's shadow can move unless he moves. Yet when Marx comes to analyse capital accumulation, we are given to understand that in England, which he takes as the prototype, the capitalist system did after all originate as a result of a new productive force, represented by the proletariat called into existence by the enclosures; though the landless beggars, to whom Sir Thomas More in his *Utopia*, and other writers of the second quarter of the sixteenth century, devote so much attention were only potentially a productive force, and to prove his case Marx would have had to show that they were absorbed into nascent industry, which he fails to do.

While therefore the theory of Marx and Engels is clear enough, they forget about it when they discuss specific modes of production, and particularly when they turn to the new order which they hope to bring about. The *Communist Manifesto* enumerates the measures that are "unavoidable as a means of entirely revolutionising the mode of production"; but although there are ten of them, including the abolition of wage labour and capital, there is no word of any change in the productive forces.[1] In his *Class Struggles in France*, Marx declares that, "Socialism is the *declaration* . . . of the class dictatorship of the proletariat as the necessary transit point to the *abolition of class distinction generally* to the abolition of the relations of production on which they rest".[2] Again, in an address given at The Hague in September 1872, he said, "One day the working class must hold political power in its hands in order to establish a new organisation of labour".[3] All

---

[1] Bober, *op. cit.*, p. 23.   [2] S.W., I, p. 203.
[3] *Corresp.*, p. 165.

therefore that the proletariat has to do is to destroy the relations of production of the bourgeoisie and take over its technology. For, as Engels puts it, "The abolition of capital *is* the social revolution and involves a change in the whole method of production".[1]

In his *State and Revolution*, Lenin makes the same assertion. "We have the right to say with the fullest confidence that the expropriation of the capitalists will inevitably result in an immense development of the productive forces of society", a development which he declares that "capitalism is already retarding to an incredible degree".[2] In fact he had no right to say any such thing. The belief, which he shared with socialists before and since, that the abolition of private enterprise will liberate the productive energies of the workers rests upon an act of faith, and experience has done little to confirm it. If, then, socialism is a new mode of production, as Marx and Engels would certainly have agreed with him in regarding it, what brings it into being is not the impact of new productive forces on the existing relations of production but a change in the relations only.

In his *Dialectical and Historical Materialism* Stalin follows the classical Marxist analysis; and as late as 1952 the short *Philosophic Dictionary* laid down that "the development of productive forces, and primarily of the instruments of production, lies at the base of change and development in the method of production of material goods". But in his *Economic Problems of Socialism in the U.S.S.R.* of the same year, it is upon the relations of production that the emphasis is now thrown. His assertion, made as far back as 1936, that the victory of socialism within the Soviet Union had been achieved, taken in conjunction with his repeated assurances that the Second World War had immensely increased Soviet power, was raising with increased insis-

[1] Letter to Cuno, Jan. 24, 1872, *Corresp.*, p. 320.
[2] S.W., VII, pp. 87–88.

tence the question as to when and how the transition into communism would be effected. In his *Economic Problems* he selects as his victim the economist N. S. Yaroshenko, who is accused of grossly overrating the role of the productive forces as the determinant of change. "The main and decisive force", Stalin now insists, are "the new production relations" that came into existence in the revolutionary period, and Yaroshenko is censured for having followed Bukharin in subordinating them to the productive forces. It is only the *old* relations of production of pre-socialist society which act as a brake upon the development of the productive forces, and the "peculiar development", as he calls it, which transforms these relations from brakes into "the principal mainspring impelling the productive forces forward" constitutes "one of the chief elements of the Marxist dialectic".[1] It is a convenient doctrine, seeing that it was he who had the last word in deciding what the relations of production were to be.

Further, Marxist theory represented production (i.e. the productive forces plus their relations) as the base, or substructure of society, upon which, as we shall see, there arose a superstructure of laws, institutions and the like. But in his *Concerning Marxism in Linguistics* (1950) Stalin re-defined the base as "the economic structure of society at a given stage of its development".[2] As this was Marx's definition of the relations of production only, the new definition meant the exclusion of the productive forces—a breach with the earlier theory that production, the basis of society, consisted of the two. At a meeting of the Soviet Academy of Social Sciences, held soon after this pronouncement, two of the participants, M. Makarova and A. I. Sokolov, rightly argued that the productive forces and their relations could not be separated, and that if the forces were excluded from production, the theory of their correspondence with the relations became meaningless.

[1] p. 70.   [2] p. 3.

It seems, however, that the majority prudently rejected this.[1]

Yet even the assumption that major changes in production are initiated by changes in the productive forces does not take us much further, as it leaves unexplained the question as to why changes in those forces should occur at all. According to Saint-Simon, progress is due to the development of technology. But while, like Marx, he makes technology the basis, he holds that its advance depends upon the emergence of men who possess the ability to make the necessary scientific inventions and discoveries, and that if such persons are not forthcoming there will be stagnation. On the other hand, Marxism teaches that once the productive forces have prepared the way for them, the inventions and discoveries will take place more or less automatically, and this is held to account for why the same ones are often made about the same time by two or more persons. A good example of this line of reasoning is given by Engels. He explains that the advance of science at the time of the Reformation was due to the new productive forces that had come into existence. The bourgeoisie, who controlled them, had need of it, and therefore supported its rebellion against the Church.[2] Yet all this is highly disputable. As F. S. Salter has pointed out, the bourgeoisie in the Marxist sense scarcely existed at the time; science and religion were not sharply opposed; while science was still too much in its infancy to be of service to the bourgeoisie in what Engels calls "the development of its industrial production".[3]

If, however, historical materialism maintains that all progress is due to purely material factors, so that inventions and discoveries are phenomena which occur when material circumstances demand them, it is, as McFadden

[1] See *Voprosy Philosfii*, No. 2, 1951, pp. 208–215.
[2] "Über den historischen Materialismus", *Neue Zeit*, 1893, Vol. II, Pt. I, p. 42.
[3] *Karl Marx and Modern Socialism*, 1921, pp. 117–118.

says, simply the old mechanistic materialism dressed up in Hegelian terminology. If, on the other hand, it recognises that progress depends on intellectual achievements, it is admitting non-material elements, and the doctrine that progress takes place as a result of the development of economic forces will have to be abandoned.[1]

* * *

The debate in which Marx (and after his death, Engels) became involved with the Russian Populists (Narodniks) provides a tail-piece to the above, for he was to find himself challenged by a party which was at least as anxious as himself to bring about a revolution, but could not see how this was possible on the basis of his analysis. What seems first to have inspired its doubts was his treatment of "capitalist accumulation", that is, his explanation of how the capitalist system arose. He had pointed out that it could not do so until there was a proletariat, and that this was brought into existence "when great masses of men are suddenly and forcibly torn from their means of production, and hurled as free and 'unattached' proletarians on the labour market". He had then explained that, "The expropriation of the workers from the soil is the basis of the whole process. . . . This history, in different countries assumes different aspects, and runs through its various phases in different orders of succession and at different periods. In England alone, which we take as our example, has it the classic form." [2] It is therefore clear that he regarded the process as normative for the development of the capitalist system, and as best illustrated by the case of England.

But in 1877 N. K. Mikhailovsky, the editor of the Narodnik periodical *Otycestvenniye Zapiski* (*Notes on the Fatherland*), published an article in which he stated that if

---

[1] *op. cit.*, pp. 234–235.
[2] *Capital*, I, pp. 736 f.; for an examination of this thesis see Goetz A. Briefs, *The Proletariat*, New York, 1937, pp. 97 f. and esp. pp. 108–110.

what Marx had said was correct, his Russian followers should be doing all they could to further the expropriation of the peasants and such other measures as would enable the country to reach the capitalist stage through which it must pass before it could achieve socialism. It was a fair deduction, as David Mitrany points out, but Marx did not like it.[1] Towards the end of the year he therefore wrote to Mikhailovsky quoting the above passage from *Capital*, but using the French edition of 1873, in which the last sentence, referring to England as exhibiting "the classic form", ends with the words "but all countries of Western Europe are going through the same movement", a statement which does not occur in any other edition, and which could be interpreted as limiting the process to Western Europe only. In his letter Marx repeated that what he had said "does not pretend to do more than trace the path by which, in Western Europe, the capitalist society emerged from the womb of feudal economy"; and in an often-quoted phrase he complained that his critic "feels obliged to metamorphose my historical sketch of the genesis of capitalism in Western Europe into an historico-philosophic theory of the *marche générale* imposed by fate upon every people".[2] But he never sent off this letter. After his death Engels forwarded it to the Narodnik leader Vera Zasulich, who published it in 1884 in one of the party organs.[3]

In 1881 Zasulich had written to Marx from Geneva. She told him of the popularity which his *Capital* enjoyed in Russia, and asked him to state plainly, for the benefit of her party, what was his attitude towards a revolution in that country. His analysis seemed to deny that it could be based on the peasant commune, and to demand that Russia must pass through the capitalist phase, and not jump a

[1] *Marx against the Peasants*, 1951, pp. 34–35.
[2] *Corresp.*, p. 353.
[3] Paul W. Blackstock and Bert. F. Hoselitz, *The Russian Menace to Europe*, 1952, p. 274.

stage in the dialectic of production. In this event, she declared, "The socialist . . . has no alternative but to devote himself to more or less ill-founded calculations in order to find out in how many decades the land of the Russian peasant will pass from his hands into those of the bourgeoisie, and in how many centuries Russian capitalism will attain perhaps a development similar to that of Western Europe".[1]

Marx was evidently much exercised by this dilemma, and among the papers preserved by his daughter, Laura Lafague, were four long drafts in which he had attempted to deal with Zasulich's enquiry.[2] The letter which he finally sent her was quite short. He interpreted the passage in *Capital* referred to above in the same way as he had done in his letter to Mikhailovsky; but as for the commune, it could only become "the strategic point of social regeneration" if it were freed from "the pernicious influence which attack it from all sides". As Mitrany says, he did not answer her question, and left it to her party to decide the matter for themselves.[3] Indeed, when Riazanov, the Director of the Marx–Engels–Lenin Institute, secured the drafts in 1911 and asked Zasulich, Plekhanov and Axelrod if they could recall Marx's reply, none of them had any recollection of it.

The probability is that they had forgotten it because it had been overlaid by Marx's letter to Mikhailovsky, and by the preface he had contributed to the Russian edition of the *Communist Manifesto* of 1882. In this preface he had declared that the commune might become "a starting point for a communist course of development", provided that "the Russian revolution sounds the signal for a proletarian revolution in the West, so that each complements the other". It was an ingenious compromise which sug-

[1] *The Russian Menace to Europe*, p. 276.
[2] They are printed in the *Marx–Engels Archiv.*, I, pp. 318–340, and are summarised by Blackstock and Hoselitz, *op. cit.*, pp. 218–226.
[3] *op. cit.*, p. 33.

gests, when taken in conjunction with his letter to Zasulich, that, in spite of his statement to Mikhailovsky, he
was not prepared to give away more of his position than
he was obliged.

As for Engels, he had anticipated Marx by declaring,
in an article, "Social Relations in Russia", which appeared in 1875, that a revolution based on the commune
might succeed "in the event of a victorious revolution
breaking out in Western Europe".[1] But in a letter to the
Narodnik economist Danielson of February 24, 1893, he
withdrew this concession. What had been said ten years
earlier was no longer true. If, he says, we had been able
to destroy the capitalist system then, it might have been
possible "for Russia to have cut short the tendency of her
own evolution towards capitalism". But this had not hap-
pened.[2] Thus when he reprinted the above article in 1894,
it was with the modification that "the initiative in such a
transformation of the Russian commune can come not
from itself, but exclusively from the proletariat of the
West".[3] When therefore in the years immediately following the October Revolution Lenin and his associates insisted that its success depended upon proletarian revolutions in the West, they were not simply thinking in terms
of the concrete situation—of a weak country which
needed the support of stronger countries—but were tacitly
admitting that although they called their revolution a
proletarian one, it was not the revolution that Marx had
prescribed.

We must not, however, conclude from this that Marx
would necessarily have disapproved of it. Undoubtedly
he took his analysis of production seriously as it was his
special contribution to socialist theory, and he was not
prepared to waive it for the benefit of a little group of

[1] Carr, *The Bolshevik Revolution*, II, pp. 388–389.
[2] *Corresp.*, p. 509; see also his letter to the same of Oct. 17, 1893, *ibid.*, p. 515.
[3] Carr, *op. cit.*, II, p. 391; cp. Blackstock and Hoselitz, *op. cit.*, pp. 283–284.

exiles whose revolutionary prospects he may well have regarded as negligible. But in the last resort what mattered was the destruction of the capitalist system, not the analysis which proved its destruction to be inevitable. He was no putschist, and did not believe that revolutions should be undertaken unless they were likely to succeed. Yet had he been in a position to view the situation in October 1917 through the eyes of Lenin, he would have seen that a party which looked to him as its prophet and enjoyed at least a fair measure of proletarian support had a good chance of making a revolution, and it is by no means certain that he would have been so unrealistic as to have said that the chance should not be taken because such a revolution did not fit into his scheme.

VI

The Class Struggle

The *Communist Manifesto* in its original version contains the famous statement that "all history is the history of the class struggle", though this was amended by Engels in the preface to the German edition of 1883 to "all history since the dissolution of the primeval communal ownership of land"; and in that of the 1888 English edition to "all hitherto existing history", that is, to history of which records exist. The sentence in the *Manifesto* which immediately follows shows that in the view of the writers, the fundamental characteristic of this struggle was the oppression of one class by another. "Freeman and slave, patrician and plebeian, lord and serf, guildmaster and journeyman, in a word oppressor and oppressed, stood in constant opposition to one another, carried on an uninterrupted, now hidden, now open fight, a fight that each time ended either in a revolutionary reconstruction of society at large, or in the common ruin of the contending classes." [1]

Engels repeatedly underlines the importance of this discovery, the credit for which he assigns, with his usual modesty, to Marx. Thus in an article on Marx, published in the Brunswick *Volkskalaender* of 1878, he declares that "Marx has proved that the whole of previous history is a history of class struggles, that in all the simple and complicated political struggles the only thing at issue has been the social and political rule of social classes and the conquest of domination by newly arising classes". But he then goes on to say, "To what do these classes owe their

[1] S.W., I, p. 33.

origin and their continued existence? They owe it to the particular material, physically sensible conditions in which society at a given period produces and exchanges its means of subsistence." [1]

Now there is a certain ambiguity here, because this identification of history with the class struggle is inconsistent with what we have already seen to be the Marxist thesis that those transformations of society which make up history are initially due to the evolution of the productive forces, and that it was this which not only led to the emergence of an exploited class and to the varying forms which its exploitation has since assumed, but also to the class struggle. If, however, the class struggle derives from this evolution, it becomes a subordinate factor in history, and our primary task will be to determine the cause of the evolution itself. If, on the other hand, as Marx and Engels constantly suggest, it has an absolute rather than a relative value because it is a dialectical process which must lead to the ultimate triumph of the class which assures the evolution of the productive forces, it is not clear how the struggle between "contending classes" can ever end with their "common ruin", as may occur according to the passage from the *Communist Manifesto* quoted above. [2]

As usual, we search in vain for any clear statement in Marx's writings as to what classes are. He devoted a brief but unfinished section to them, inserted by Engels at the end of Vol. III of *Capital*, yet neither there nor elsewhere did he attempt to explain at all fully what he meant by them. The nearest approach that he makes to a definition is that which he gives of the French peasants in his *Eighteenth Brumaire* (1852): "In so far as millions of families live under economic conditions of existence that separate their mode of life, their interests and their culture from those of

[1] S.W., II, p. 149.
[2] J. Delevsky, *Antagonismes sociaux et antagonismes prolétariens*, Paris, 1924, pp. 58–59, 63.

other classes, and put them in hostile opposition to the latter, they form a class. In so far as there is merely a local inter-connection among these small-holding peasants, and their identity of interests begets no community, no national bond and no political organisation, they do not form a class." [1] As he held that, despite their common interests, these peasants showed no disposition to unite, he did not regard them as a class, but rather, as he puts it, as "a sack of potatoes". For, in his view, identity of interests, that is, of economic interests, forms the basis of a class, upon which there develops a class-consciousness which expresses itself in a variety of opinions which its members share; and it was because he saw no signs of this development among the French peasants that he rejected them as a class, though this did not prevent him from treating the peasantry in general as a class in his later writings.

In his letter of the same year to Georg Weydemeyer, Marx pointed out that he did not pretend to have discovered the class struggle, which had already, he said, been analysed by "bourgeois" historians and economists, Thierry and Guizot being cited among the former and Ricardo among the latter.[2] What he did claim to have demonstrated was, "(1) that the existence of classes is only bound up with *essential historical* phases of the development of production; (2) that the class struggle necessarily leads to the dictatorship of the proletariat; (3) that

[1] S.W., I, p. 303.
[2] In a letter to Engels of July 27, 1853, Marx says that he has been reading with great interest Thierry's *Histoire de la formation et du progrès du tiers état* (1853). He calls Thierry "the father of the class struggle in French historiography", but remarks that it was singular that in his preface he should have attacked "the moderns" for holding the class struggle to be one between the bourgeoisie and the proletariat, of which traces were to be discerned in the French Revolution, and for representing it (as indeed Guizot had also done) as one between the *tiers état* and the privileged noblesse and clergy, the former being held to embrace all sections of society with the exception of the latter. Marx's criticism is that Thierry fails to see that the struggle has changed it character because the bourgeoisie is now no longer opposed to the above sections, with which it has made common cause. (*Briefwechsel*, Stuttgart, 1913, II, p. 34.)

this dictatorship only constitutes the transition to the *abolition* of all classes and to a classless society".[1] The meaning of the first of these discoveries is that classes are not phenomena which belong to the established order of nature, but that they only come into existence with the development of production, and assume a form determined by that development. For although Marxist–Leninists resent the charge that they only attach importance to economic factors, it is to these alone that they turn when they have to deal with classes. A man's class is not determined by what he may believe it to be, but by the position he occupies within a given system of production. Thus Lenin defines classes as "large groups of people who differ from each other by the place they occupy in an historically definite system of social production, by their relations to the means of production, by their role in the social organization of labour, and consequently by the dimensions and methods of acquiring the share of the social wealth which they obtain".[2] Yet this is scarcely a satisfactory definition. For if it is his relation to a system of production that determines the class of the factory worker, that relation will be the same whether his factory is run by private enterprise or by an omnipotent State, the only difference being that he is likely to be better off under the former than under the latter.

Marx admits, as indeed he has to do, that society is made up of a multiplicity of classes. But for the purpose of his dialectical analysis, they had to be reduced to two only, and it is therefore his thesis that any society can ultimately be broken down into a class which owns or controls the means of production and a class which does not, though this cleavage does not become clearly marked until a system of production has become well-established. The

---

[1] March 5, 1852, *Corresp.*, p. 57. For a well-documented treatment of the Marxist doctrine of the class struggle see H. Bartoli, *La doctrine economique et sociale de Karl Marx*, 1950, pp. 309 f.

[2] *A Great Beginning*, June 1919, S.W., IX, pp. 432–433.

effect of the capitalist system has been, however, to sim-
plify this division, so that society now consists of the bourgeoisie on the one hand and the proletariat on the other.
As Engels points out, the two are inter-dependent, as the
bourgeoisie cannot exist without the proletariat or the proletariat without the bourgeoisie.[1] None the less, the interests of the two are irreconcilable, and those of the proletariat are destined to prevail.

In the *Communist Manifesto* the term "bourgeoisie" is
used in the sense in which it was originally employed by
the French, that is, for the class engaged in industry and
commerce—the "burghers" who grew up in the later
Middle Ages alongside the feudal lords. In current English usage it means the "middle-class", but as communist
writers invariably use the designation Marx and Engels
gave it, it will be convenient to follow their example. The
Manifesto specifically identifies it with the ownership of
capital, and with the power to "exploit" which this confers. "In proportion as the bourgeoisie, i.e. capitalism, is
developed, in the same proportion is the proletariat, the
modern working class, developed." But in his *Anti-Dühring*, written many years later, Engels shifts the attack.
The bourgeoisie has now become the non-producing class.
It no longer performs any useful function, and the sole
activity of its members is to clip dividend coupons and
gamble on the Stock Exchange.[2]

This at least implied some recognition of the fact that
there had come into existence a managerial class of sal-
aried employees whose members did not owe their control over production to the possession of capital, which
was now for the most part vested in a body of passive
shareholders, the majority of whom were small investors.
To argue that such persons can no longer be described as
capitalists, at least in the earlier sense, may seem to be a
quibble. But when we are told that the bourgeoisie has

[1] *Anti-Dühring*, p. 24.   [2] p. 312.

"pitilessly torn asunder" the ties that formerly held men together, and has left nothing save "naked self-interest and callous 'cash payment' ", we are entitled to be told who it is that behave in this manner. Do they include, for example, such persons as mill-owners, of whom Engels was one until he sold his share of the family business and joined that rentier class which he denounced? And how is the professional class to be fitted into this scheme? Marx and Engels would certainly have regarded its members as bourgeois, though they may have no capital whatever.[1] Communist propaganda represents them as parasites whom the capitalist bourgeoisie proper—Marx's "upper ten thousand"—has called into existence to render it various services; but this will not do, since even if they could be shown to be parasites, it would not follow that they were bourgeois unless their class is to be defined in much wider terms than communists employ.

The Marxist conception of the bourgeoisie suffers in fact from the defect common to the whole system of using a single factor to explain a highly complex phenomenon. What distinguishes the bourgeoisie as a class is not that its members own capital, but that they tend to recognise a certain common standard of values which derive largely from their education and upbringing. Of course the possession of money may play a part in creating these values; but it is a far cry from this to the statement that members of the bourgeoisie are what they are because they own or control the means of production. Communist theoreticians have long recognised this, and have given the term such an extension as will enable them to attack "bourgeois" literature, art and philosophy as class products alien to the proletarian mind. No attempt is made to represent the writers, artists and philosophers as capitalists in the formal sense, though it is main-

[1] For a Marxist examination of his question see Rudolf Schlesinger, *Marx. His Time and Ours*, 1950, pp. 216–223.

tained that their work reflects the capitalist system and supports it.

We find the same imprecision when we turn to the proletariat. Charles Andler has observed that "the whole critical effort of Marxism" is to establish its existence, since once it has been established all the conclusions it is desired to draw readily follow.[1] Yet we are left without any exact definition; and it was not until the English edition of the *Communist Manifesto* of 1888 that Engels inserted a footnote explaining that the proletariat was "the class of modern wage-labourers who, having no means of their own, are reduced to selling their labour power in order to live"—a definition which requires only slight terminological changes to apply equally to a large section of the bourgeoisie. Certainly it is a late-comer on the political stage since, according to Engels, it was not until 1830 that it emerged, and then only in England and France, as an element ("a third competitor for power") in the class struggle, which had hitherto lain between the bourgeoisie, as the representative of the *tiers état*, and the aristocracy.[2] Yet although he and Marx sometimes convey the impression that it embraces all the "toiling masses", they do in fact exclude from it whole groups of workers, and specifically the peasants (the earliest of all producers) and the "down and outs" (*Lumpenproletariat*), to whom they refer invariably with contempt, though it is these unfortunates above all who "have nothing to sell but their labour power", whereas the proletarian worker may own his own house and have a comfortable balance in the savings bank without forfeiting his class status.

In fact, the term "proletarian" early came to be narrowed down to the urban industrial worker, who is brought by the nature of his employment into close

---

[1] *Le Manifeste Communiste*, Paris, 1901, pp. 63–64. For an interesting discussion of the concept as a whole and of Marx's treatment of it see François Jeanson, "Définition du Prolétariat", *Esprit*, July–Aug. 1951, pp. 1–22.

[2] *Feuerbach*, S.W., II, p. 356.

contact with others of his kind, and is thus the more class conscious and easier to organise than other branches of labour. Marx and Engels hold it to be "the only *really* revolutionary class", that is, the only class whose interests are antithetically opposed to those of the bourgeoisie. In the *Communist Manifesto* "the small manufacturer, the artisan and the peasant" are lumped together as "fractions of the middle class" which the proletariat will eventually absorb, since, as they must be assigned to one or the other of the two classes, it is convenient to dismiss them as anomalies destined to disappear with capitalism. At the same time, Marx and Engels have to take them into account when they come to analyse the class structure of any particular society with a view to determining what role its various elements would play in the event of revolution. Here the petty-bourgeoisie, as represented by "artisans and shopkeepers", come in for hard treatment as a reactionary class. "They will", says Engels, "always remain the same. They hope to climb, to swindle their way into the big bourgeoisie; they are afraid of being dragged down into the proletariat." Were a revolution to take place they would therefore remain neutral, and join the winning side when it was over. "Such", he declares "is their nature." He adds that they are "extremely unreliable". The *Lumpenproletariat* is even more unsatisfactory; "This scum of the depraved elements . . . which establishes its headquarters in the big cities is the worst of all possible allies. This rabble is absolutely venal and absolutely brazen." [1]

The peasants constituted a more serious problem, and one which cannot be discussed in detail here. Marx and Engels regarded them as a reactionary class because they owned land and desired only to have more of it. Further, both were obsessed with the belief that peasant farming,

---

[1] Preface to *The Peasant War in Germany* (1874), S.W., I, pp. 583-584; cp. Marx, *The Class Struggles in France, ibid.,* p. 142.

perhaps the best of all its forms, was doomed, and that the future lay with large-scale agriculture—a belief which Stalin shared until he became disillusioned in the middle thirties.[1] Marx, indeed, had based his social analysis upon the industrialised West, and was therefore inclined to regard the peasants as relatively unimportant. Yet as early as 1848 Engels had noted that the territories between the Baltic and the Black Sea could only be emancipated by an agrarian revolution; and the problem of the form which a revolution in such areas should take was to exercise Marx when he was later called upon to advise the Russian Narodniks as to whether a new social order could be based upon the peasant commune.

Marxism was thus hostile to the peasants, as were in consequence those socialist parties which adopted Marxist programmes. But this confronted such parties with a dilemma. Had Marx's prognosis been correct, the peasants could have been safely ignored as a declining class, whereas it had become clear by the end of the century that, so far from diminishing, their number and the size of their holdings had actually increased. There could indeed be no justification for admitting to the party a class whose interests Marx had declared to be antagonistic to those of the proletariat. Yet it must not be converted into an enemy, for, as the German Social-Democratic leader Wilhelm Leibknecht, had observed, "We do not need the peasants to make a revolution, but no revolution will stand if the peasants are against it".[2] In *The Peasant Question in France and Germany* (1894), the most complete analysis of the peasant situation before Lenin, Engels examines in turn the rich landowners, the farmers and smallholders on the one hand, and the agricultural labourers, whom he calls "rural proletarians", on the other. He stresses the importance of the peasants as an element in

[1] David Mitrany, *Marx against the Peasant*, 1951, pp. 27–28.
[2] *op. cit.*, p. 33.

the class structure, and notes their suspicion of socialism and of anything which suggested the domination of the town over the countryside. But he was still convinced that they had no future. They should not be threatened with expropriation, or forced into that co-operative farming wherein lay their salvation. Yet nothing should be done to encourage them to suppose that they could permanently retain their dwarf holdings.

After the failure of the 1905 revolution Lenin saw, however, that tactics demanded a change of policy towards the peasants. In his *Agrarian Programme of Social Democracy* (1905) he distinguished, as Engels had done, between peasant proprietors and landless farm workers, the former being a reactionary class, while the latter were "semi-proletarians" and belonged to the working class.[1] But in his *Agrarian Question in Russia* (1908) he made his classical analysis of the peasants into rich peasants who employed labour, poor peasants who owned nothing, and middle peasants who farmed with their own labour, but were being gradually driven down into the ranks of the poor peasants. He now argues that the peasants as a class are the natural allies of the proletariat in a revolution,[2] a discovery which the *Short History of the CPSU* tendentiously assigns to his *What "The Friends of the People" Are* of 1894.[3] But this alliance does not signify that the two classes have a "single will" apart from their common interest in the destruction of Tsarism, for in his *Two Tactics* of 1905 he points out that after the victory "it will be ridiculous to talk about 'singleness of will' of the proletariat and the peasantry, about a

---

[1] S.W., I, pp. 141f.; III, pp. 166 f. In his *Report on Work in Rural Districts*, March 1919, Lenin admits that Engels was the first to make this distinction, S.W., VIII, p. 173.

[2] Actually Lenin took over this idea from Marx, who had pointed out in his *Eighteenth Brumaire* that the fragmentation of the land by Napoleon had reduced the peasants to such a state of degradation that they now "find their natural ally and leader in the *urban proletariat*, whose task is the overthrow of the bourgeois order". S.W., I, p. 306.

[3] p. 14.

democratic dictatorship etc. When that time comes, we shall attend to the question of the proletarian dictatorship . . ." [1] It was on this alliance of the "whole peasantry" with the proletariat that the so-called "bourgeois-democratic" February Revolution was based, after which the slogan was changed to that of "the dictatorship of the proletariat and the poor peasants"—the slogan of the October Revolution. According to Stalin, the two shared the leadership until the breach between the Bolsheviks and the Social Revolutionaries took place in 1918 "when it passed *wholly* and *entirely* into the hands of our Party".[2] For communist theory teaches that the proletariat is the leader in any revolution, and that it must not share its power with any other class. It alone represents the interests of the masses, and its will is their will.

It is therefore understandable that the rise of the Chinese Communist Party under Mao Tse-tung and its eventual triumph should have excited the apprehension of Moscow. That the October Revolution was proletarian and the architype of all future revolutions was an article of faith, and on it rested Moscow's claim to direct the world-revolutionary movement. To admit that Chinese communism was a peasant movement was to concede to it a character of its own, for its revolution would be a peasant revolution, and one to which the principles which govern the proletarian variety would not necessarily apply. But Mao was careful to preserve appearances. He called his party proletarian even when it was not, and he shifted its centre of gravity back to the cities as soon as this became feasible. The Chinese revolution has certainly led to a more realistic awareness of the importance of the role of the peasants, particularly in countries which are still primarily agricultural. Yet it is still the accepted

[1] S.W., I, pp. 405–406.
[2] Stalin, "The Party's Three Fundamental Slogans on the Peasant Problem", 1927, *Leninism*, ed. 1940, pp. 180–182.

doctrine that any revolution, even one of the bourgeois-democratic and non-socialist type, must be under proletarian leadership.

For Marxism rests on the belief that the proletariat is the bearer of the idea of progress, that its subordinate status is only a transitory phenomenon and that its evolution is that of mankind itself. Marx was to offer an economic justification for this view. But it had been held by more than one eighteenth- and early nineteenth-century thinker. That men should be willing to fall upon one another despite their common nature was due to the character of the society which divided them. All who possess property are condemned to an eternal, fratricidal struggle. The proletariat alone is uncorrupted, and in it alone there is true brotherhood. Hence it is its mission to restore society to its pristine innocence. The proletariat is good because it is not tainted by that original sin which lies in the assertion that "this field is mine". Behind the harsh world of competition there is Humanity, and the proletariat constitutes Humanity. This is the myth of the proletariat. It is a myth because there is no true proletarian any more than there is a Nature- or Reason-inspired man. But it served the proletarian cause, until in time the proletariat became dissolved in the Party, for which it is no longer Humanity, but simply the raw material of a planned society which the world is to be compelled to accept.[1]

It is then the propertyless masses, represented in classical Marxist–Leninist theory by the proletariat, that have always been, as the Soviet Academician G. F. Alexandrov declared, "the creators of history and the motive force of social progress".[2] Hence Soviet historians are required to show that whatever period they may be writing about illustrates a conflict between this progressive element and one which is reactionary, in which task they are assisted

[1] E. Berl, *La Culture en Peril*, Paris, 1948, pp. 238 f.
[2] Moscow broadcast of Nov. 7, 1953.

by the looseness of the class-struggle concept, which makes it possible to represent almost any event as a manifestation of it. Yet even if the role attributed to it in the transition from feudalism into capitalism be granted, the assumption that it played a similar one in earlier stages of history rests upon an act of faith. The rivalry between the patricians and the plebeians in republican Rome was not due by any means solely to economic considerations, and there were wealthy men in both parties.[1] Certainly the class structure of the later Roman Empire underwent changes by no means beneficial to society. Yet the breakdown of that Empire, and with it of the slave economy which Marxism regards as its essential feature, is not attributable to a struggle between two classes for the control of the means of production analogous to that between the rising bourgeoisie and the declining feudal landowners. Certainly Marx produces no evidence to the contrary. "The class struggles of the ancient world", he observes, "took the form chiefly of a contest between debtors and creditors, which in Rome ended in the ruin of the plebeian debtors. They were displaced by slaves."[2]

Again, the transition from slavery into feudalism was not due to a struggle between masters and slaves in which the latter had been the victors. The slaves did not become the feudal lords in the new society.[3] Nor did the class struggle determine the feudal economy. When the feudal conqueror settled land upon his more important followers, his object was to create an elementary form of administration rather than an economic system. That in time feudal landlordism developed, and the landlords came to constitute a class is undeniable; but to satisfy the Marxist thesis, the feudal system should have arisen as a result of a conflict between two classes, and for this no proof is forth-

[1] Henri Sée, *Matérialisme historique et l'interprétation économique de l'histoire,* Paris, 1927, pp. 101–102.
[2] *Capital,* I, p. 112; but cp. Stalin, *Leninism,* ed. 1940, p. 457.
[3] Bober, *op. cit.,* pp. 338–39; Delevsky, *op. cit.,* pp. 119 f.

coming. Indeed, Engels virtually abandons the whole case by conceding that under feudalism classes arose from political causes, and that it is only in "modern history" that "all political struggles are class struggles" [1]: while Lenin, on the authority of the *Origin of the Family*, admits that at certain periods the class struggle has not determined the course of political events, and instances the dynastic age of the seventeenth and eighteenth centuries.[2] As for the class relations of feudalism, the *Communist Manifesto* had already declared them to have been "patriarchal and idyllic", which scarcely suggests a conflict.[3] Indeed, Engels tells us that in the Middle Ages the producer owned the product of his labour "as a matter of course". He had made it himself, and even if he had used outside help, this was "as a rule subsidiary". He does not regard the guild apprentices and journeymen as victims of exploitation, since they "worked less for the sake of their board and wages than to train themselves to become master craftsmen". But in this event, there can have been no class struggle.[4]

As Schumpeter says, Marx's contribution is an important one if his statement in the *Communist Manifesto* is toned down to mean that historical events may often be interpreted in terms of class interests and class attitudes, and that existing class structures are always an important factor in historical interpretation.[5] But his doctrine goes far beyond the recognition of this which, as he himself admitted, was already acknowledged by many of his contemporaries. In his treatment of classes he uses his habitual technique of appealing to familiar facts to support conclusions that by no means necessarily follow from them. Classes are not only represented as engaged in

---

[1] *Feuerbach*, S.W., II, pp. 356–357.
[2] *The State and Revolution*, S.W., VII, p. 14.
[3] S.W., I, p. 35.   [4] *Anti-Dühring*, p. 303.
[5] Joseph A. Schumpeter, "The Marxian Doctrine", in *Capitalism, Socialism and Democracy*, 1943, p. 14.

an incessant struggle, but in a struggle which has a meaning, since it is predestined to end with the victory of the proletariat, though why it must do so is never established. So, again, his version of the relation between classes underlines all the elements that divide them and ignores all those that make for solidarity; while he refuses to recognise the fluidity of the class structure, and assumes that every member of a class will have the same interests, whereas these may well agree with those of another class on certain points and be opposed to them on others.[1] Yet it is undeniable that the relation between classes is normally one of collaboration, as the divergencies between them are transcended by a higher common interest, seeing that it is to the advantage of both parties to maintain production, just as, to quote T. H. Marshall's illustration, "the bowler and the batsman have a common interest in enabling one another to play cricket, though their views as to the most desirable fate of every ball bowled are diametrically opposed".[2]

What, however, we are justified in saying is that where an economic system leads to the emergence of two recognisably distinct groups, conflicts will arise between them, and will create tensions that have to be resolved. But these conflicts do not arise, as Marx asserts, on account of the contradictions inherent in the system itself, so that they were inevitable however it had been organised. A potent source of them is the conviction in the mind of the workers that the system that employs them is fraudulent, and Marx did more than any other man to foster this with his doctrine of surplus value, according to which the worker is exploited whatever wages he receives. Apart from this, their primary cause is the abuse of power. When Engels wrote his *Condition of the Working Class in England*, and indeed for many years after, it was the owners of capital

[1] Delevsky, *op. cit.*, pp. 308 f.
[2] *Citizenship and Social Classes*, 1951, p. 117.

who had this power, and it was only gradually that it was brought under control, partly by legislation and partly by labour organising itself until the workers were able to contract with their employers on terms which are now often more favourable to the former than to the latter. The result was to weaken the element of class conflict, and strengthen that of class solidarity, as Engels ruefully admitted.[1] But the measures which brought about this state of affairs were supported in England by a large section of middle-class opinion; and in countries where that class shows no adequate sense of social responsibility, a class struggle in the Marxist sense is likely to develop.

If, however, Marx's statement is to be regarded, as undoubtedly he wants it to be, as a law which applies to all periods of history, we may agree with Croce that it is only true (a) when there are classes, (b) when they have antagonistic interests, and (c) when they become aware of this antagonism. For Croce points out that there have been societies in which there has been no determinate class structure, that classes have not always had antagonistic interests, and that they have often been unaware of them, of which the propaganda designed to create the antagonism is an admission. And, as he adds, history will presumably go on, even in a classless society.[2]

Yet if the Marxist thesis is correct, it is not clear how it can do so. As Marx puts it, "From the very moment in which civilisation begins, production begins to be based on the antagonism of orders, of states, of classes, and finally on the antagonism between capital and labour. No antagonism, no progress. This is the law which civilisation has followed down to our own day." [3] It would seem, therefore, that with the classless society, in which there is no longer any antagonism, the dialectic of history must

---

[1] See his preface to the 1892 edition of *Condition of the Working Class in England*, S.W., II, p. 376.

[2] *Historical Materialism and the Teaching of Karl Marx*, pp. 85–86.

[3] *The Poverty of Philosophy*, pp. 65–66.

come to an end. Neither Marx nor Engels face the problem as stated in these terms. But in somewhat different contexts Engels rejects this conclusion. "If", he declares "at any time in the evolution of mankind such a final, conclusive system of the inter-connections within the world—physical as well as mental and historical—were brought to completion, this would mean that human knowledge had reached its limit and, from the moment when society has been brought into accord with that system, further historic evolution would be cut short—which would be an absurd idea, pure nonsense." [1] And again: "Just as knowledge is unable to reach a complete conclusion in a perfect, ideal condition of humanity, so is history unable to do so: a perfect society, a perfect 'State', are things which can only exist in imagination".[2] With this we may well agree. Yet it is not easy to reconcile it with the Marxist dialectic. For if that conflict, which is stated to be essential to progress, only takes the form of a struggle between classes, and if this is made the subject-matter of history, the elimination of classes, and thus of the conflict, must logically be the end of history, and not, as is contended, its beginning.

The Leninist answer is that such a conclusion rests upon a "mechanistic" identification of antagonism with contradiction. All antagonisms are contradictions, but not all contradictions are antagonisms. As M. Shirokov explains, "Antagonistic contradictions are resolved by the kind of leap in which the internal opposites emerge as relatively independent opposites, by a leap that leads to the abolition of the formerly dominant opposite and to the establishment of a new contradiction", in which "the subordinated opposite of the previous contradiction now becomes the dominant opposite"; whereas in non-antagonistic contradictions, "the development of the contradiction

[1] *Anti-Dühring*, p. 46.
[2] *Feuerbach*, S.W., II, p. 328.

signifies not only the growth of the forces making for its final resolution, but each new step in the development of the contradiction is at the same time also its partial resolution".[1]

What this means, the reader must decide for himself. We are, however, to understand that in a class-divided society the contradictions which arise between classes are antagonistic, whereas in a socialist society there will be no such contradictions because there will be no longer any antagonism. But this does not mean that there will be no contradictions. For, as Lenin puts it, "Antagonism and contradiction are by no means the same. Under socialism the first will vanish; the second will remain. If in developed socialism there were no contradictions—contradictions between productive forces and relations in production, between production and demand, no contradictions in the development of technique, etc.—then the development of socialism would be impossible, then instead of movement we should have stagnation. Only in virtue of the internal contradictions of the socialist order can there be development from one phase to another and higher phase."[2]

Stalin reaches a similar conclusion. Even under socialism there will still be contradictions between the productive forces and the relations of production, because the development of the latter always tends to lag behind that of the former. He adds, however, that "given a correct policy on the part of the directing bodies", such contradictions "cannot grow into antagonisms" or lead to a conflict between the forces and the relations, though, were a wrong policy to be pursued, "a conflict would be inevitable" and might seriously obstruct the development of the productive forces.[3]

[1] *Textbook of Marxist Philosophy*, n.d., pp. 174–175.   [2] *ibid.*
[3] *Economic Consequences of Socialism in the U.S.S.R.*, p. 75.

VII

The Substructure and the Superstructure

In his speech at Marx's graveside Engels declared that: "Just as Darwin discovered the law of development of organic nature, so Marx discovered the law of development of human history: the simple fact, hitherto concealed by an overgrowth of ideology, that mankind must first of all eat, drink, have shelter and clothing, before it can pursue politics, science, art, religion, etc.; that therefore the production of the immediate material means of subsistence and consequently the degree of economic development attained by a given people or during a given epoch form the foundation upon which the state institutions, the legal conceptions, the ideas on art, and even on religion, of the people concerned have been evolved, and in the light of which they must, therefore, be explained, instead of vice versa, as had hitherto been the case." [1]

Here Engels is laying down three propositions. The first seems an obvious one—that unless men can support themselves, they cannot engage in politics, science and the like because they would all be dead. The second declares that this "simple fact has been hitherto concealed by an overgrowth of ideology", and that Marx was the first to clear it away. The third, which is the really important one, is that "the level of production" is "the foundation" of the various forms the above activities take, and "in the light of which they must therefore be examined".

Had Engels been asked to give his authority for attributing these opinions to Marx, he would doubtless have referred his enquirer in the first instance to the preface to

[1] S.W., II, p. 143.

the *Critique of Political Economy*, in which Marx drew his celebrated distinction between the substructure and the superstructure of society. As to what constitutes the substructure there is indeed a certain ambiguity, for we are first told that the relations of production are "the economic structure of society", and that upon this there arises "a legal and political superstructure" which corresponds to "definite forms of social consciousness": and in the next sentence, that it is the mode of production, of which the relations are only a part, that "conditions the social, political and intellectual life process in general", which last is again the superstructure, though it has now been given a wider extension.[1] It is then explained that when the mode of production changes, the superstructure does the same. For it is by changes in the substructure that transformations in society are effected, not by changes in the superstructure, since the elements of the latter, which Marx calls "ideological forms", are simply reflections of the former, so that when the one changes, the other "is more or less rapidly transformed".[2]

Although the preface to the *Critique of Political Economy* first clearly formulates this division of social phenomena into substructural and superstructural, the thesis had already been adumbrated in Marx's earlier writings. In his *Eighteenth Brumaire* he declares that, "Upon the different forms of property, upon the social conditions of existence, rises an entire superstructure of distinct and peculiarly formed sentiments, illusions, modes of thought and views of life. An entire class creates and forms them out of its material conditions and out of the corresponding social relations".[3] Even earlier the *German Ideology* had laid

---

[1] In the *German Ideology* the productive forces together with the relations of production are also represented as constituting the substructure. "The sum of productive forces . . . and social form of intercourse . . . is the real basis of what the philosophers have conceived as "substance" or "essence of man". M.E.G.A., Abt. 1, Bd. 5, p. 28; Eng. trans., p. 29.

[2] S.W., I, pp. 328–329.

[3] S.W., I, p. 247.

down that "empirical observation must in every separate instance bring out without any mystification or speculation the connection of the social and political structure with production"; while the same writing had drawn attention to the fact that in every epoch, "the class which has the dominant *material* power in society is at the same time the dominant *spiritual* power", so that "the dominant ideas are nothing but the ideal expression of material conditions".[1] This is again emphasised in the *Communist Manifesto*, "What else does the history of ideas prove than that intellectual production changes its character in proportion as material production changes. The ruling ideas of every age are those of its ruling class." [2]

What, then, Marx is saying is: First, that ideas, or at least those that he calls ideologies, are derivatives of the economic substructure. Secondly, that both the ideas and the various forms in which they find expression are devised in the interests of whatever is the class that controls the existing economic order. Thirdly, that neither the ideas nor the forms they assume can thus claim, as the *German Ideology* puts it, "any semblance of independence". They do not exist in their own right, but are ideologies— false and misleading ideas, which profess to give an explanation of reality, but are on examination simply the reflection of class attitudes and class interests. Fourthly, that in considering changes in society, "a distinction should always be made between the material transformation of the economic conditions, which can be determined with the precision of natural science, and the ideological forms in which men become conscious of the conflict and fight it out". The former are the primary determinants of change; the latter are only secondary.

According to the *German Ideology*, the superstructure

[1] M.E.G.A., Abt. I, Bd. 5, pp. 15, 35; Eng. trans., pp. 13, 39.
[2] S.W., I, p. 49; cp. the *German Ideology*, M.E.G.A., Abt. I, Bd. 5, p. 35; Eng. trans., p. 39.

emerges with that division of labour which gives rise to classes, but which only becomes a "real division" when physical and mental labour are separated from one another, that is, when the activity of thought becomes divorced from that of material production, "so that it emancipates itself from the world, and passes on to the formation of 'pure theory', of theology, philosophy, morals etc.".[1] For at a certain stage in the development of the productive forces a sub-class makes its appearance whose members, because they are not engaged in production proper, excogitate constructs which either bear no relation to reality, or are at best inadequate representations of it. In his *Anti-Dühring*, Engels argues that it is this that brings into existence a governing class, "Side by side with the great majority, whose lives are devoted to the burden of production, there arises a class freed from it, which takes charge of the common affairs of society—the direction of labour, justice, science, arts etc.".[2] Such a division of labour will no longer exist under communism. It might be supposed that even in a classless society the artist, scientist and judge will have to be released from physical labour if they are to work as they should, but we shall see later that Marx and Engels hold that this is not at all necessary, as once capitalism has been destroyed, it will be possible for anyone to combine any number of different activities. Yet we need not wait for communism to abolish this division, since, according to Stalin, it has already disappeared in the Soviet Union, though he interprets it simply as "the gulf which under capitalism divided the physical workers from the managerial personnel", which Marx and Engels would have regarded as only a single aspect of it.[3]

The ideologies which the *German Ideology* assigns to the superstructure are specifically theology, morals, philo-

---

[1] M.E.G.A., Abt. I, Bd. 5, p. 21; Eng. trans., p. 20.   [2] p. 316.
[3] *Economic Problems of Socialism in the U.S.S.R.*, p. 31.

sophy and law. To these Marx adds in the preface to the *Critique of Political Economy* politics and aesthetics; while Engels declares that "politics, law, philosophy, literature, art etc." are all "based on economic development", and thus fall into the same category".[1] In his *Feuerbach* Engels says that the Middle Ages "knew no other form of ideology than precisely religion and theology",[2] but he contradicts this later in the same writing by maintaining that "the state presents itself as the first ideological power over mankind", and that it produces a further ideology, since "it is among the professional politicians, theorists of public law and jurists of private law that the connection with economic facts is completely lost".[3] This would seem to attribute a primacy to law and politics, both of which existed long before the Middle Ages. At the same time Engels recognises that there are ideologies which are "still higher" than these because they are "further removed from the economic base", so that although all are ideologies, some are more ideological than others.

Thus the position would seem to be that society is divided into those who are not engaged in physical labour, but think and, as a result, produce ideologies, and those who are engaged in it, and do not think at all, but simply accept the ideas current at the time; though this is scarcely consistent with the constant assertions that the proletariat has discovered the falsity of the ideology of the bourgeoisie and has rejected it. But the French sociologist, Georges Gurvitch, argues that in the *German Ideology* Marx and Engels make *some* ideas, namely those belonging to what they call "the language of real life", a part of that "total living sensuous activity" which they blame Feuerbach for having failed to understand,[4] and that they distinguish such ideas from the products of

[1] Letter to Heinz Starkenburg, Jan. 25, 1894, *Corresp.*, p. 517.
[2] S.W., II, p. 344.
[3] S.W., II, p. 359.
[4] M.E.G.A., Abt. I, Bd. 5, p. 34; Eng. trans., p. 36.

"spiritual production" which are ideologies.[1] What, however, Gurvitch overlooks is that they both recognise one field of ideas which is not ideological because their truth can be tested by empirical methods, and it is presumably these that belong to "the language of real life". The theory of evolution, for example, presents us with certain concepts about the origin, nature and development of man, but they are not ideological in so far as they claim to be supported by scientifically ascertainable facts; whereas, morals, philosophy and art are ideologies because they rest upon presuppositions about goodness, truth and beauty which are not scientifically verifiable. It will be noted how sharply Marx distinguishes in the preface to the *Critique of Political Economy* between changes in the economic conditions, "which can be determined with the precision of natural science", and the "ideological forms", which cannot be.

For while Marx and Engels hold that the science of every age has been influenced by the prevailing ideology, they do not hesitate to make use of the conclusions of bourgeois scientists, and do not regard science itself as an ideology. The same is true of Stalin, who does not include it in his *Concerning Marxism in Linguistics* among the ideologies, that is, among those things that a revolution would liquidate. Commenting upon this writing, the philosopher, F. V. Konstantinov, declared that while the social sciences were superstructural, the natural sciences were mainly independent of classes; [2] though this is not accepted by the majority of present-day Soviet propagandists, to judge from their continual attacks upon western science.

The view that ideas are superstructural and stem from

[1] "La sociologie de Marx" in *La vocation actuelle de la sociologie*, Paris, 1950, p. 596 f.
[2] "The Development by Comrade Stalin of Marxist–Leninist Theory regarding the Basis and the Superstructure", *Izvestiya Akademii Nauk SSSR, History and Philosophy Series*, No. 3, 1951, pp. 209–220.

the economic base—that is, from production—has given rise to much controversy, as it is clearly one which can be given a wider or narrower interpretation. It may only mean that the ideas of an age, and the forms in which they are expressed, will be such as a given "degree of economic development" is capable of producing, so that we do not find in a primitive society those which characterise a highly industrialised civilisation; or that it is the "degree of economic development" which actually decides the nature of the ideas and forms; or some position intermediate between the two. As the first of these explanations is tautological, we may assume that it would not have satisfied Marx and Engels, and the question is therefore how much further they intended to go. But this is one which cannot be answered, because they restrict themselves to generalisations, and never give specific examples of how superstructural elements are formed out of the substructure. As, however, they had committed themselves unreservedly to the assertion that all such elements were determined by it, it was only natural that many of their followers should have concluded that the relation between them was one of cause and effect, as if, as Charles Andler puts it, the Sermon on the Mount was deducible from the economic conditions of first-century Palestine, or the religion of the apostles from their occupation as fishermen or tent-makers.[1]

If, however, we are to show that production is responsible for the superstructure, we must be able, as H. B. Acton points out, to separate the two, and find something which is production, but which contains nothing superstructural whatever; and this would only be possible on the assumption that no legal, political, moral or other superstructural elements enter into production at any point, though they clearly play an important part in deciding the form

---

[1] "La conception matérialiste de l'histoire", *Revue de la Métaphysique et de la Morale*, 1907, p. 656.

that they had both been "equally guilty" of deriving ideologies and actions arising as a result of them from "basic economic facts", and of emphasising the content of these actions rather than "their formal side, the ways and means by which they come about". In these and other letters of this series he concedes further that just as the substructure acts upon the superstructure, so does the superstructure act upon the substructure, though he invariably concludes by declaring the substructure to be the decisive factor. Yet such statements as that "the mode of production basically determines a culture in the last instance" cannot be accepted unless the terms "basic" and "the last instance" are defined.[1] Moreover, if we are to call the economic factor "basic", we must explain what we mean by "economic", and any attempt to do so inevitably ends by introducing elements which are not. And to admit an interaction between the substructure and the superstructure is to destroy the whole case. For to make the substructure ultimately responsible for the forms which the superstructure assumes does not make sense once it has been conceded that the substructure is only what it is because of the influence upon it of the very things it is alleged to determine.

The more enlightened Marxists of the second generation were not unaware of these difficulties. Plekhanov points out that a knowledge of the economic life of eighteenth-century France will not explain the origin of the minuet, but holds that it was none the less "the expression of the class psychology of the non-producing class". What the connection is he does not tell us, and, as Hook says, "the psychology of the non-producing class" could have been expressed just as well by a dance of a quite different character.[2] Similarly, Kautsky argues that although society is governed by economic forces, they do not account for this

---

[1] Sidney Hook, *Reason, Social Myths and Democracy*, p. 128.
[2] *Towards an Understanding of Karl Marx*, pp. 157–158.

or that social phenomenon. "It was", he says, but without being more explicit, "an economic revolution that brought about a spiritual awakening in Greece, and another economic revolution that caused its decline." But this does not mean that the forms of Greek art were due to economic causes.[1] Yet if they were not, the theory loses all its significance, and is reduced to the innocuous statement that the economic substructure determines everything in general but nothing in particular.

Bernstein has observed that there are many passages in the writings of Marx and Engels which prove that they were aware of the influence of non-economic forces.[2] Only, as he rightly says, we are dealing here with a question of proportion—not with whether ideological forces are admitted, but with the influence to be attributed to them; and it cannot be denied that even after Engels had sought to adjust the balance, the role they are given is a secondary one only, since although inter-action is conceded, no example is ever given of a change in society effected by a non-economic force against the wishes of the class that controls production. Yet in fact Marx and Engels were in a dilemma. Either production had to be interpreted in such a way as to include all forms of social reality, in which case their fundamental thesis could not be sustained; or they had to adopt such a restricted definition of it as would support that thesis, and shut their eyes to the awkward fact that it was the very factors they had excluded that made it what it was. It was upon this second alternative that they eventually decided.[3]

Historical Materialism in challenging the received opinion that the world is governed by ideas went to the opposite extreme, as is common with reactions, and denied that they had any effective influence. Yet if economic

---

[1] "Aims and Limitations of the Materialist Conception of History", *Social Democracy*, Feb. 15, 1903, pp. 100–101.
[2] *op. cit.*, p. 11.   [3] Gurvitch, *op. cit.*, pp. 601–602.

conditions are not a sufficient explanation of the religious, moral and philosophical and other ideas of society, they are certainly necessary to a full understanding of them. In his *Holy Family* Marx asks, "Do these gentlemen think that they can understand the first word of history so long as they exclude the relations of man to Nature, natural science and industry? Do they believe that they can actually comprehend any epoch without grasping the industry of the period, the immediate methods of production in actual life?" This is perfectly reasonable, and its implications contain the element of permanent value in the doctrine. It insists, as Herbert Butterfield reminds us, that every historical movement must be viewed in the context of the social structure, and that all human activities, even the highest achievements of the mind, have their roots in material conditions. Yet this can be held without denying the existence of a spiritual element, as it simply defines the kind of universe in which the spirit works. The doctrine is thus a corrective to the view which regards history as the field of activity of disembodied ideas, existing apart from men and human needs.[1] But while this is indeed true, it does not make the form in which the doctrine is presented any the less untenable.

Certainly Stalin did nothing to render it more acceptable. In his *Dialectical and Historical Materialism* he does not specifically mention the substructure and the superstructure, but declares that the source of ideas is to be found "in the conditions of the material life of society", or what he calls its "being", and that it is upon these conditions that the ideas of any period depend. But this, he says, accounts only for "*the way they arise*", and does not mean that they are unimportant, seeing that "it is impossible to carry out the urgent tasks of the development of the material life of society without . . . their transforming action". This is simply Marx's teaching as revised by

[1] "Marxist History" in *History and Human Relations*, 1951, pp. 66 f.

Engels. Marx had represented the superstructure as no more than a complex of ideologies. But in his *Concerning Marxism in Linguistics*, Stalin declared it to be an "exceedingly active force" which is created by "the base" or substructure "precisely in order to serve it" by assisting to destroy the older and moribund superstructure, and thus "give free scope to the development of the productive forces of society". Yet a few paragraphs later we are told that it "is not directly connected with production, with productive activity", but only "indirectly" through the base, that it reflects changes in production only *after* these have led to changes in the base, and that its sphere of action is thus "narrow and restricted".[1] But if this be so, it is not clear why it should possess the importance that he evidently desires to attribute to it.

This writing was greeted with the usual roar of acclamation, and all its commentators were agreed that its peculiar merit lay in its recognition of the role of the superstructure, though Engels had already stressed this, while pointing out that it could stand in a number of relations to the substructure, whereas Stalin only recognises one—that of service.[2] In fact the primacy attached by Marx and Engels to the material economic conditions remains unchallenged. D. I. Chesnokov declares without qualification that "any part of the superstructure is wholly and completely determined by the base";[3] and while P. S. Trofimov was so bold as to assert that the "great realistic art" of the past (and the same, he said, was true of literature) was "related to the people", and was therefore not superstructural, it would appear that he was voicing the opinion of a minority of Soviet philosophers only.[4]

[1] pp. 4, 7.
[2] Letter to Heinz Starkenburg, Jan. 25, 1894; *Corresp.*, pp. 516 f.
[3] "The Place of the State in the System of the Superstructure", *Proceedings of the Academy of Sciences of the U.S.S.R., Izvestiya Akademii Nauk SSR*, Sept.–Oct. 1951.
[4] *Voprosy Filosofii*, No. 2, 1951.

VIII

The State

At the time when Marx and Engels began to interest themselves in revolution it was generally accepted by advocates of social change that the state was an external power set over its subjects, and not an agency which represented them, as it could scarcely be said to do in any country. Hence there were many who believed that it should be replaced by some form of "association". As to precisely what this would be, there were differences of opinion, but it was held to imply a self-governing society in which there would be no longer any need for repression. Thus Marx declares in *The Poverty of Philosophy* that in place of "the old order of civil society" the working class will set up "an association which excludes classes and their antagonism";[1] while the *Communist Manifesto* looks forward to the day when "social power will lose its political character", and all production be "concentrated in vast association of the whole nation".[2] The notion that the social order of the future would be thus constituted persisted after the Bolsheviks came into power, and in addressing the first American Labour Delegation in 1927 Stalin made "the free association of toilers" one of the characteristics of a communist society.[3]

Marx retained throughout his life a deep distrust of the state, and Engels equally shared it. As the *German Ideology* declares, it is "nothing more than the form of organisation which the bourgeoisie necessarily adopts both for internal and external purposes for the guarantee of its

[1] p. 100. [2] S.W., I, p. 35.
[3] *Leninism*, ed. 1933, II, p. 70.

property and interests".[1] It was an evil which must be destroyed as being essentially the expression of the contradiction in society between the haves and the have-nots. At the same time, he never swerved from his conviction that the economic transformation of society, which was the ultimate object of the revolution, could not be achieved unless the proletariat first obtained political power, and that even after the revolution, the state, with its machinery of coercion, would have to be retained for a time in order to crush all survivals of the old order. For this he provided with his doctrine of the dictatorship of the proletariat, the significance of which will be considered later. Thus he neither agreed with the anarchists, who held the destruction of the state to be the sole object of the revolution, nor with the anarcho-syndicalists, who adopted Proudhon's teaching, of which Sorel later became the exponent, that the activity of the proletariat should be restricted to the economic field only.

It is, however, to Engels rather than to Marx that we are indebted for an exposition of these views. They are most systematically set forth in his *Anti-Dühring*, (1878), and *The Origin of the Family, Private Property and State* (1884). But both writings may be regarded as expressing the views which they held in common. For Marx not only wrote one chapter of the section of *Anti-Dühring* which deals with economics, but allowed Engels to read the whole text to him in manuscript, and presumably listened with some attention, since the refutation of Dühring, who had been perverting their best disciples Wilhelm Liebknecht and August Bebel, was an important operation; while *The Origin of the Family*, which appeared shortly after his death, was based, as already noted, upon their joint study of Morgan's *Ancient Society*, to the thesis of which Engels added some touches of his own. As, however, the latter deals with the origin of the

[1] M.E.G.A., Abt. I, Bd. 2, p. 52; Eng. trans., p. 59.

state, and the former with what is to happen to it, it will be convenient to take them in that order.

Engels starts with the assertion that the state is not a natural institution. "It has not existed from all eternity. There have been societies which managed without it, which had no conception of the state or of state power." [1] In primitive, or gentile, society there did indeed exist some rudimentary organisation which looked after "the common affairs of its members", but this, he says, was not a state, as "it had no coercive power except public opinion", which was homogeneous, as there were no "internal antagonisms" within society. What possible proof there can be of this is not stated. It is then argued that the state comes into existence with the breakdown of this society in order to protect the property of the individual against collective ownership. "At a definite stage of economic development, which necessarily involves the cleavage of society into classes, the state became a necessity because of the cleavage." "The state is a product of society at a certain stage of development. It is the admission that society has become entangled in an insoluble contradiction with itself, that it is cleft into irreconcilable antagonisms that it is powerless to dispel. But in order that these antagonisms, classes with conflicting interests, may not consume themselves and society in sterile struggle, a power apparently standing above society becomes necessary, whose purpose is to moderate the conflict and keep it within the bounds of 'order'; and this power, arising out of society, but placing itself above it, and increasingly separating itself from it, is the state."

The latter part of the last sentence should be noted, as it suggests that the state is primarily the product of society, and only in the second instance that of class divisions within it, a view which contains interesting implications to which we shall return. In his *Feuerbach* it is set out even

[1] *The Origin of the Family*, S.W., II, p. 293.

more explicitly; "Society created for itself an organ for the safeguarding of its general interests against external and internal attacks. This organ is the state power. But hardly has this organ come into being than it makes itself independent in regard to society, and indeed the more so as it becomes the organ of a particular class".[1] In his *Origin of the Family*, Engels expressly says that the organisation set up by gentile society to look after its "common affairs" was not a state, but it would now appear that at some stage or another society did establish one, and that it was then captured by the dominant class, though elsewhere in the same writing we are told that this last only happens "as a rule",[2] which would seem to be a further admission that it is possible for a state to exist without being a class organ at all.

For what we may call the metaphysic of the state we must turn to *Anti-Dühring*. Here at least Engels makes clear that he regards the state simply as the product of class antagonism, so that it will logically disappear when there are no more classes. This thesis he expounds in what is perhaps the most famous passage in his writings: "*The proletariat seizes the state power, and transforms the means of production in the first instance into state property*. But in doing this, it puts an end to itself as the proletariat, it puts an end to all class differences and class antagonisms, it puts an end also to the state as a state. Former society, moving in class antagonisms, had need of the state, that is, an organisation of the exploiting class at each period for the maintenance of its external conditions of production. . . . The state was the official representative of society as a whole, its embodiment in a visible corporation; but it was this only in so far as it was the state of that class which itself, in its epoch, represented society as a whole; in ancient times, the state of the slave-owning citizens; in the Middle Ages, of the feudal nobility; in our epoch of the bour-

---

[1] S.W., II, p. 358.   [2] *ibid.*, p. 290.

geoisie. When ultimately it becomes really representative of society as a whole, it makes itself superfluous. As soon as there is no longer any class of society to be held in subjection; as soon as, along with class domination and the struggle for individual existence based on the former anarchy of production, the collisions and excesses arising from these have been abolished, there is nothing which would make a special repressive force, a state, necessary. The first act in which the state comes forward as the representative of society as a whole—the taking possession of the means of production in the name of society is its last act as a state. The interference of the state power in social relations becomes superfluous in one sphere after another, and then ceases of itself. The government of persons is replaced by the administration of things and the direction of the process of production. The state is not abolished, it withers away."[1]

What, then, we may regard as the classical Marxist doctrine is that the state arose when society became divided into classes, and that its characteristic feature is coercion exercised over the majority through the army as a "public force" "separated from the mass of the people", and through the police and the machinery of justice, all of which the minority are alleged to control. There will thus be no longer any need for it in the classless society. This is how both Lenin and Stalin understand the matter. "The state", Lenin declares, "is the product of the irreconcilability of class antagonism. It arises when, where and to the extent that class antagonisms *cannot* be objectively reconciled."[2] Stalin is equally explicit. "The state arose because society split into antagonistic classes. It arose in order to keep in restraint the exploited majority in the interests of the exploiting minority."[3] And again: "The

---

[1] p. 315.
[2] *The State and Revolution*, S.W., VII, p. 8.
[3] Report to the Eighteenth Congress (1939), *Leninism*, ed. 1940, p. 660.

state is primarily a weapon of one class against another class. Thus it follows quite clearly that as soon as there are no classes there will also be no state." [1] It is a theme to which both constantly return, and no purpose would be served in multiplying citations in which they express the same view in almost identical terms.

Marx had believed at first that it was only necessary that the proletariat, which would constitute at the time of the revolution the immense majority of the population, should disarm what was left of the capitalist bourgeoisie and take over the apparatus of government. The experience of the Commune, which he held to be the prototype of the proletarian revolution, led him to revise this opinion, and in the preface which he and Engels jointly contributed to the 1872 edition of the *Communist Manifesto* they declared that "the working class cannot simply take hold of the ready-made state machine and wield it for their own purposes". Lenin describes this as the only amendment to the *Manifesto* that Marx and Engels ever made to it,[2] and that they regarded it as important is attested by the satisfaction with which Engels recorded in a letter to Bernstein that the Russians had shown a very proper feeling by incorporating it into their translation.[3] Lenin bitterly complains that Bernstein had twisted it into a warning to the proletariat not to display too much revolutionary zeal.[4] But Marx did not mean this, as Bernstein doubtless knew perfectly well; for in a letter to Dr. Kugelmann of April 12, 1871, he refers to the last chapter of his *Eighteenth Brumaire* (1851), where he had said that "the next attempt of the French Revolution will be no longer, as before, to transfer the bureaucratic-military

---

[1] *Speech to the Seventh Plenum of the E.C.C.I.*, Dec. 13, 1926, *Works*, IX, pp. 129–130.
[2] *The State and Revolution*, S.W., VII, p. 35.
[3] Jan. 1, 1884. *Briefe von Friedrich Engels an Eduard Bernstein*, Berlin, 1925, pp. 134–135.
[4] *The State and Revolution*, VII, p. 98.

state machine from one hand to another, but to smash it".[1] The error of the Commune had been its failure to do this. At the same time, it had introduced a number of ultra-democratic devices, some of which Lenin was later to adopt; and in their introduction Marx and Engels expressed their approval of them.

Marx's version of the Commune is contained in his *Civil War in France* (1871); and when a re-edition of this appeared in 1891, Engels contributed an introduction, in which he refers to what they had both said in 1872. "What", he asks, "had been the characteristic of the former state? Society had created its own organs to look after its common interests, originally through simple division of labour. But these organs, at whose head was the state power, had in course of time, in pursuance of their own special interests, transformed themselves from the servants of society into the masters of society." He goes on to point out that "It is precisely in America that we have the best example of the growing independence of state power in opposition to society, whose mere instrument it was originally intended to be".[2]

This is a return to the view expressed in the passages from *The Origin of the Family* and *Feuerbach* referred to above, in which the state is represented as something which society creates, but which then tends to become a law unto itself.[3] But this may well provide the basis of an entirely different theory. For if the state only becomes the "master" of society when it is annexed by whatever may be the dominant class, it should no longer constitute a danger once it has become proletarian, provided the necessary safeguards are introduced to prevent it from becoming once again an organ of oppression. Engels maintains

---

[1] *Corresp.*, p. 309.
[2] S.W., I, pp. 438–439.
[3] Marx seems also to have held that as the state develops it tends to become increasingly separated from society; see *The Civil War in France*, S.W., I, p. 469.

that the election of all officials by universal suffrage and the right of recall provide "two infallible expedients" for guaranteeing its social character, though when it was proposed to introduce similar measures into the Gotha Programme of 1875, Marx contemptuously brushed them aside as being no more than "the old familiar democratic litany". If, however, what Engels says is correct, the force of the argument that the state must disappear because it is in itself an evil is seriously weakened.

Yet it is certain that Engels had no wish to weaken it. His last word on the subject is to be found in the above introduction to the *Civil War in France*; "People think that they are making an extraordinarily big step forward when they rid themselves of faith in a hereditary monarchy and become partisans of a democratic republic. In reality, however, the state is nothing more than a machine for the oppression of one class by another, in a democratic republic no less than in a monarchy. At best the state is an evil, inherited by the proletariat after coming out victorious in its struggle for class supremacy. The victorious proletariat, just like the Commune, will be obliged immediately to amputate the worst sides of this evil, until such time as a new generation, brought up under new and free social conditions, will prove capable of throwing all this state rubbish on the dust-heap." [1]

In the treatment by Marx and Engels of their basic concepts there is nothing dialectical at all. They are endowed with certain essential qualities, and their nature is unchanging. So it was with the state. What they had said of it continued to find an echo in the Latin countries, where it was traditionally suspect; but the conclusions which were drawn were not their own, but those of Proudhon, and later of Bakunin. On the other hand, there existed in Germany a traditional respect for the state, exhibited in

---

[1] S.W., I, pp. 439–440; cp. his letter to Philip von Patten, April 18, 1883, *Corresp.*, pp. 416–417.

Lassalle's *étatisme*, which Marx had viewed with grave misgivings. When therefore the Lassalleans amalgamated with his own followers in 1875 at the Unity Congress of Gotha, one of his most devastating criticisms of the new party's draft programme was "the riotous misconceptions it created with regard to the state", which it treated as "an independent entity", and not as "an organ super-imposed upon society" and destined to disappear; [1] while Engels urged that "the whole talk about the state be dropped", and the term be replaced by *Gemeinwesen* (Community), "a good old German word which can very well reflect the French *commune*".[2] They failed to carry their point, and it was not until the Erfurt Congress of 1891 that the party adopted a thorough-going Marxist programme, which committed it to the destruction of the "bourgeois state". None the less, the leaders found themselves driven by circumstances to make use of it to obtain benefits for the workers; and it was this policy that led to the revisionist controversy, associated with Bernstein—an issue which was taken up by all the continental parties and divided them until war was declared in 1914.

Up to the eve of the October Revolution, Lenin had steered a middle course, rejecting alike the tendency to compromise with the bourgeois state and the anarchist objection to states in general. But, as Robert V. Daniels has pointed out, he had hitherto shown little interest in the relations of the state to a proletarian revolution, or in those writings of Marx and Engels in which this problem had been discussed.[3] For the opinions later expressed in *The State and Revolution* he was indebted to Bukharin, and also to Anton Pannekoek, who may well have been Bukharin's source of inspiration. Pannekoek, a distinguished

[1] *Critique of the Gotha Programme*, S.W., II, pp. 29–30.
[2] Engels to Bebel, March 18–28, 1875, *Corresp.*, pp. 336–337.
[3] "The State and Revolution. A Case Study in the Genesis and Transformation of Communist Ideology", *American Slavic and East European Review*, Feb. 1953, pp. 25 f.

astronomer, was one of the leaders of the Dutch left-wing socialist group known as the "Tribunists", and was closely associated with Rosa Luxemburg's group in the German party. In 1912 he entered into controversy with Kautsky, and published three articles in *Neue Zeit*, entitled "Mass Action and Revolution",[1] to which Kautsky replied; and in January 1916 he contributed to a Swiss left-wing periodical, *Der Vorbote*, a further article, "Imperialism and the Tasks of the Proletariat", in which he reiterated his earlier arguments, and contended that "the struggle of the proletariat is, in the first instance, a struggle *against the state power*".[2]

Lenin did not at this time share Pannekoek's extremist opinions, but during the First World War the two were drawn together on the basis of their common opposition to the attitude that Kautsky was adopting. At the end of 1916, however, his attention was drawn to some articles which Bukharin had contributed to the *Jugendinternationale*, and in particular to one which had appeared in its issue of December 1, entitled "The Imperialist Robber State", in which, under the *nom de plume* of "Nota Bene", he had enlarged upon Pannekoek's thesis. In this he had argued that the classical Marxist doctrine that the collapse of capitalism would inevitably lead to socialism required to be revised in view of the fact that capitalism had entered upon the era of imperialism. For it was now possible that the state would become a collective capitalist, in which event the workers might well find themselves even more exploited than ever. Hence he contended, as Pannekoek had done, that the fundamental task of the proletariat was to smash (*sprengen*) the bourgeois state, which was now even more dangerous than when Marx had said that it must be destroyed.

[1] XXXII, pp. 541 f., 585 f., 609 f.
[2] Prior to its publication in *Der Vorbote* it had been printed in *Kommunist*, a Russian periodical edited by Bukharin, of which one double number only was issued in Geneva in 1915.

Lenin's reaction to this article was that in his unquali-
fied demand for the destruction of the bourgeois state
Bukharin was veering dangerously in the direction of
anarchism, and years later, when Stalin was compassing
his downfall, this charge against him was revived.[1] For
Bukharin, so Lenin complained, had made no mention of
Marx's insistence that even after the revolution the coercive functions of the state would have to be retained;
while in his *Anti-Dühring* Engels had not said that it was
to be smashed, but that it would gradually disappear.[2] But
during the winter he embarked on the study that was to
take shape as *The State and Revolution*, and he now went
back to the articles of Bukharin and Pannekoek, incorporating the destruction of the bourgeois state into
his revolutionary programme, and appealing for his
authority to what Marx and Engels had said in their
introduction to the 1872 edition of the *Communist Manifesto*.[3] This accorded, as Daniels points out, with the views
of the revolutionary idealists who constituted the left-
wing of the party. At the same time Lenin secured all he
wanted by emphasising that over "a whole epoch" the
powers of the state must continue to be exercised in the
form of the dictatorship of the proletariat. He was willing
to concede with Engels that it would "wither away", and
doubtless he believed that it would eventually do so. In
the meantime it was essential that it should be preserved
and strengthened. Indeed, in his *Can the Bolsheviks Retain*

[1] "The Right Deviation of the C.P.S.U.", *Leninism*, ed. 1940, pp. 276 f.
[2] S.W., V, pp. 243–244.
[3] A note on p. 284 of Vol. II of Lenin's miscellaneous writings (*Leninskii
Sbornik*), published in 1924 under the editorship of Kamenev, specifically
declares Bukharin's article to have been the source of *The State and Revolution*.
But Lenin also went back to Pannekoek's articles against Kautsky, as he not
only devoted the last section of his pamphlet to that controversy, but also
pp. 368–379 of the notebook he compiled before he set to work upon it, entitled "Marxism and the State" (*Leninskii Sbornik*, XIV, pp. 208–385), in
which, while not fully accepting Pannekoek's formulation, he minimises his
disagreement with him in order the better to express his disapproval of
Kautsky (see Daniels, *op. cit.*, pp. 25–29).

State Power? (1917) he comes very near to admitting that once the state has become proletarian the classical objections to it are no longer valid. "The state is an organ or apparatus of force to be used by one class against another. So long as it remains an apparatus for the bourgeoisie to use force against the proletariat, so long can the slogan of the proletariat be only—the destruction of the state. But when the state has become an apparatus of force to be used by the proletariat against the bourgeoisie, then we shall be fully and unreservedly for a strong state power and centralism." [1]

The dictatorship of the proletariat as described in *The State and Revolution* closely follows the regime set up by the Commune, which Lenin had always taken as his model. The administration of the state and of production was to be transferred to the workers. No official was to receive more than "workers' wages", and all were to be subject to recall. But, as E. H. Carr points out, little of this revolutionary ideology survived the years of "War Communism". It was not that Lenin had changed his theories. What had changed was the political and economic situation. The revolution had led to consequences that its authors had never anticipated, and they soon found themselves confronted with famine, civil war and foreign intervention. In such circumstances, the question of the destruction of the bourgeois state became an academic one, since the real problem was to devise a form of government which would maintain some semblance of order. The workers had proved unequal to the tasks imposed upon them, and thus, so far from destroying the existing apparatus, Lenin found himself obliged not only to retain the greater part of it, but also to call upon the services of the Tsarist officials, who were alone competent to run it, though this excited strong opposition within the party.[2]

It was above all in these years that Lenin laid himself

[1] S.W., VI, pp. 276–277.   [2] *op. cit.*, I, pp. 245 f.

open to the charge of first acting and then finding the required justification in a distortion of Marxist theory. That he was a supreme opportunist cannot be denied, and indeed he owed his supremacy in the party to his unerring eye for the right tactical solution, which again and again brought back to his side men who had broken with him, but who came to see that it was he and not they who had judged correctly. He possessed all the inhuman qualities of the revolutionary fanatic, for whom nothing matters save the attainment of the goal. For such men, power is a necessity. It was, as Lenin himself declared, "the fundamental question of the revolution".[1] Yet he did not seek it for the sake of personal aggrandisement, nor is it likely that he would have tolerated that adulation which his successor made no attempt to check, and presumably welcomed. But such a demand for power is not incompatible with the conviction that the object of the revolution was to build up a society based on certain principles, though if any of them stood in the way, it might have, at least temporarily, to be sacrificed, just as the social-democrat, Posadovski, had insisted at the 1903 Congress that the democratic principles for which his party stood must be considered exclusively from the standpoint of whether or not they assisted it—a view which Plekhanov continued to hold even after he had joined the Mensheviks.[2] In the period that succeeded Lenin's rise to power, the over-riding consideration was to save the revolution, and to him this could only mean the Bolshevik Party must save it. Thus the party and the state became identified, with consequences which were to be disastrous.[3]

Stalin at first sheltered behind the authority of Lenin, of whom he claimed to be no more than the interpreter. The dictatorship of the proletariat, now declared to be the

[1] *On Slogans*, July 1917, S.W., VI, p. 171.
[2] Ian Kucharzewski, *The Origins of Modern Russia*, New York, 1948, pp. 470–473.
[3] Isaac Deutscher, *The Prophet Armed. Trotsky:* 1879–1921, 1954, pp. 335–336.

centre of Marx's teaching, was the only genuine form of democracy, though it must be exercised through the party, as Lenin had insisted at the Tenth Congress of 1921. Yet with the passage of years the contradiction between its allegedly provisional character and its ever-increasing powers inevitably called for explanation. Stalin first modified the doctrine of the "withering away" of the state in his Report to the Sixteenth Congress of 1930. "We are in favour of the state dying out, and at the same time we stand for the strengthening of the dictatorship of the proletariat, which represents the most powerful and mighty authority of all forms of state which have existed up to the present day. The highest possible development of the power of the state with the object of preparing the conditions of the dying out of the state. Is this 'contradictory'? Yes, it is contradictory. But this contradiction is a living thing, and completely reflects Marxist dialectics." [1]

Thereafter Stalin developed three main lines of defence. First, it was necessary to retain and strengthen the state on account of the danger of capitalist encirclement; and indeed as long as the danger persisted, it would have to be retained, even when the transition into communism within the Soviet Union had been effected. Since the division of the world into two camps, each of which has fundamentally antagonistic interests, is simply the extension to the international field of the conflict between the national bourgeoisie and its proletariat, it could be argued that the non-socialist camp was bent upon the destruction of the Soviet Union. Yet in this event it followed equally that the Soviet Union aspired to destroy the non-socialist camp. This, however, was a con-

---

[1] *Leninism*, ed. 1933, II, p. 402. The source of this particular piece of nonsense may well have been a passage in Marx's *Eighteenth Brumaire*, quoted by Lenin in *The State and Revolution*, in which he says that the state machine must be perfected before it can be destroyed, and that its perfecting is the task of the first phase of the revolution (S.W., I, p. 301).

clusion that it was felt injudicious to draw, as it would be an admission of the true character of Soviet policy, whereas it was considered desirable to exhibit the Soviet Union as the champion of world peace.

Secondly, the state is necessary on account of the persistance of bourgeois survivals. This argument became less effective when Stalin, in introducing the 1936 Constitution, declared that the victory of socialism within the Soviet Union had been achieved, and that there were no longer any antagonistic classes, as this might reasonably have been accompanied by a relaxation of the state's internal powers. Indeed, if the Soviet system is all that it claims to be, so that, as Stalin put it in his Report to the Eighteenth Congress of 1939, "the humblest Soviet citizen being free from the fetters of capitalism . . . stands head and shoulders above any high-placed foreign bigwig whose neck wears the yoke of capitalist slavery", it is not easy to see why anyone thus happily situated should continue to be attracted by a system so inferior to his own, and need to be so carefully guarded against its pernicious influence.[1]

Thirdly, the state is the main instrument for bringing about those material and moral changes which the transition into communism demands. This was the thesis which Stalin laid down in a somewhat casual fashion at the Eighteenth Congress, though it was evident that he intended it to be taken seriously, as every commentator at once acclaimed it as a revelation which had raised the Marxist–Leninist theory of the state to a new and higher level. For if the Soviet state is the state of the working class, and must therefore by definition promote its interests, the stronger it becomes, the more fully will those interests be promoted. Hence those who object to its increasing power must be opposed to the revolutionary

---

[1] Abraham Brumberg, "The Soviet Campaign against Survivals of Capitalism", *Russian Review*, April 1953, p. 75.

cause. That the state will disappear sooner or later is indeed accepted by all Soviet theoreticians. Like the Second Coming, it will take place in the fullness of time. Meanwhile, it is a matter about which the faithful are not to ask embarrassing questions.

IX

The Society of the Future

It has been said of Marx that he set off in search of socialism and discovered capitalism, and this is true in so far that the greater part of his theoretical writings is devoted to its analysis. As to what would replace it, neither he nor Engels have much that is positive to tell us, and indeed, as Hayek points out, both they and their followers discouraged as "unscientific" any enquiry into the working of the socialist order, which would be governed by new factors, since those determining economic activity in the present would have disappeared.[1] As Engels declared, "We are not called upon to construct utopian systems about the construction of the new society." "To speculate", he says, "on how a future society might organise the distribution of food and clothing leads directly to utopia." [2] For revolutions are acts of faith, and it was not Marx's business, or at least so Lenin maintains, "to make idle guesses about what cannot be known", but rather for "the *experience* of the mass movement to provide the reply to the question of the exact forms the organisation of the proletariat will assume, and the exact manner in which this organisation will be combined with the most complete and consistent 'winning of the battle of democracy' ".[3]

Certainly Marx had nothing but contempt for the blueprints of his contemporaries, which he regarded as calculated to raise false hopes among the proletariat and

[1] F. A. Hayek, *Collectivist Economic Planning*, 1935, p. 13.
[2] *The Housing Problem*, S.W., I, p. 572; cp. p. 568.
[3] *The State and Revolution*, S.W., VII, p. 39; cp. p. 46.

weaken its revolutionary zeal. In his *Poverty of Philosophy* (1847) he had pilloried the "humanitarians" who sought "to palliate existing conditions", and the "philanthropic school", which was the "humanitarian school perfected"; [1] and in the *Communist Manifesto* he attacked in succession all the rival versions of socialism. [2] In his *Class Struggles in France* (1850) "doctrinaire socialism" is accused of seeking to wish away the revolutionary class struggle by means of "petty artifices and gross sentimentalities"; [3] and in his *Eighteenth Brumaire* (1852) he complains again of "doctrinaire experiments, exchange banks and workers' associations". [4] He did not support labour political movements or trade unions because he believed that the workers would gain any substantial benefits from them, but because they were the means through which class consciousness was created, and were therefore training grounds for revolution. Thus he approved the Co-operative movement in England, as it showed that the workers were capable of organising themselves and of defeating the capitalists on their own ground. Yet he warned the "Working Men's International Association" that co-operative labour "however excellent in principle . . . will never be able to arrest the growth in geometrical progression of monopoly, to free the masses, nor even perceptibly to lighten the burden of their miseries". [5]

In the socialist society of the future there will be of course no more classes. But what ultimately differentiates it from the present capitalist society is not so much that it is classless, but that it is one that is for the first time organised upon a rational principle, which becomes possible only when private enterprise has been abolished, and with it the class division of society. For, according to the Marxist economic analysis, the worker is not only

[1] pp. 13–136. [2] S.W., I, pp. 51–60.
[3] S.W., I, p. 203. [4] S.W., I, p. 232.
[5] Oct. 1864, S.W., I, p. 348.

exploited under the capitalist system because a part of the value he creates is withheld from him by his employer in the form of profits, but also, for this very reason, recurrent economic crises are inevitable, as the home market is unable to absorb the commodities that are produced and are then offered to those who cannot afford to buy them. It was useless to attempt to reform the system; and the only way of ensuring that the resources of society were developed to their utmost capacity was to transfer them to the proletariat as the one class which has no interest in profit-making and is concerned only with full production.[1]

For Marx and Engels, therefore, socialism implied a planned economy which would replace what they continually refer to as "the anarchy of social production"; and this was reasonable enough, since if the self-adjusting planning which takes place under the capitalist system is to be abolished, the need for an alternative is evident. In a course of lectures delivered at Elberfeld as early as 1841, Engels explains that under capitalism there is a disequilibrium between production and consumption, whereas in a communist society it should be easy to establish a ratio between the two, and thus "to fix in advance how much of any article is required for the needs of the people".[2] The *Communist Manifesto* is somewhat more explicit, as we are told that "the proletariat will use its political supremacy . . . to centralise all instruments of production in the hands of the state, i.e. of the proletariat organised as the ruling class", and that state factories will be extended and improved "according to a common plan".[3] To place the burden of planning production squarely on the shoulders of the state would seem, indeed, the obvious solution, and in fact collectivism inevitably leads to state capitalism. But Marx and Engels were inhibited from accepting this save as a temporary expedient, as they were com-

[1] H. J. Blackham, *The Human Tradition*, 1953, pp. 121–123.
[2] M.E.G.A., Abt. 3, Bd. I, p. 373.   [3] S.W., I, pp. 50–51.

mitted to the belief that the state would disappear, and that production would thereafter be "concentrated in the hands of a vast association of the whole nation". As to how it would then be organised they do not say.

It is of interest to compare with the above the catechism, drafted by Engels in 1847, for which the *Communist Manifesto* was substituted. To Question XIV, "What form should the new order take?", he replies that, "The exercise of industry and of all branches of trade will be taken out of the hands of private individuals, competing against one another, and be handed over to society which will use them for the common good on the basis of a common plan and with the participation of all members of society. It will therefore suppress capitalism and substitute association"; and to Question XX, "What will be the consequence of the suppression of private industry?", that the transference of the productive forces from private hands and their administration "according to an established plan" will remove all the evils associated with large-scale industry, and that economic crises will thus disappear. No proof is offered of the truth of either statement.[1]

There is an equal insistence upon planning in Engel's later writings. "Only the conscious organisation of social production, in which production and distribution are carried on in a planned way, can elevate mankind above the rest of the animal world."[2] With the transference of the means of production to society "anarchy in social production is replaced by systematic, definite organisation".[3] "The proletariat seizes power . . . and socialised production upon a predetermined plan becomes henceforth possible."[4] "The social productive forces are only waiting for the proletariat to take possession of them in order to

[1] *Grundsätze des Kommunismus*, M.E.G.A., Abt. I, Bd. 6, pp. 511, 516–517.
[2] Preface to the *Dialectics of Nature*, ed. 1930, p. 19.
[3] *Socialism, Utopian and Scientific*, S.W., II, p. 140.
[4] *ibid.*, p. 142.

bring about a state of things . . . which so increases their yield by the planned operation of the whole of production that the satisfaction of all reasonable needs will be assured in an ever increasing measure." [1] But it is in the section on socialism in his *Anti-Dühring* that this matter receives its fullest treatment. Here again he speaks of "the replacement of the anarchy of social production by a socially planned regulation of production in accordance both with the needs of society as a whole and of each individual" [2]; of "society making itself master of the means of production in order to use them in accordance with a social plan" [3]; and of the "social act" as a result of which "society, by taking possession of the means of production and using them on a planned basis, has freed itself and all its members from the bondage in which they are now held". [4] When this comes about, it will be possible to calculate without any difficulty the quantity of social labour embodied in a given commodity, and "people will be able to manage very well without the intervention of the famous 'value' ". [5]

The instrument through which this transformation is to be effected is once again the state. "The proletariat seizes the state power and transforms the means of production in the first instance into state property." Only this, as we have seen, is its last independent act as a state, for it then disappears. [6] Thus Engels pronounces against state capitalism, as "the modern state, whatever its form, is essentially a capitalist machine", so that "the more productive forces it takes over . . . the more citizens it exploits". "State ownership is not the solution of the conflict, but it contains within itself the formal means, the handle to the solution." [7] In his *Economic Problems of Socialism in the U.S.S.R.* Stalin endorses this. "Conversion into state pro-

[1] *Karl Marx*, 1878, S.W., II, p. 152.
[2] p. 314. [3] *ibid.*, p. 328. [4] *ibid.*, p. 355.
[5] *ibid.*, pp. 345–346. [6] *ibid.*, p. 315. [7] *ibid.*, p. 313.

perty is not the only, or even the best form of nationalisa-
tion, but its initial form, as Engels says in his *Anti-Dühring*",
for the ultimate goal is "society itself in the shape of a
central directing economic body".[1] He does not tell us
what we most want to know—how this body will be constituted, and wherein it will differ from a state, seeing that
it will have presumably to enforce its decisions. Lenin had
indeed laid down that "by what stages, by what practical
measures, humanity will proceed to this higher aim—we
do not and cannot know".[2] Yet if this be so, it is surely
presumptuous to assert that it will ever be attained.

Marx is of the same opinion as Engels. "A new social
order is possible in which . . . through the planned utili-
zation and extension of the existing productive forces . . .
the means of existence, for enjoying life, for the development and employment of all bodily and mental faculties
will be available in an equal measure and in ever increasing fullness".[3] In the *Inaugural Address of the Working Men's
International Association* (October 1864) he contrasts "the
blind rule of the supply and demand laws, which form
the political economy of the middle class" with "social
production controlled by social foresight, which forms
the political economy of the working class";[4] for as he
told Kugelmann, "The point of bourgeois society consists precisely in this, that *a priori* there is no conscious
social regulation of production".[5] He held that the
Commune had sought to replace "the constant anarchy
of capitalist production" by a form of production that
would "regulate material production upon a common
plan", and if such a system became operative, "what
else", he asks, "would it be but Communism?"[6] The
same idea recurs in the section on political economy
that he contributed to *Anti-Dühring*, in which he says that

[1] p. 76. [2] *The State and Revolution*, VII, p. 91.
[3] *Wage Labour and Capital*, S.W., I, p. 73.   [4] S.W., I, p. 347.
[5] July 11, 1868, *Letters to Kugelmann*, 1934, p. 74.
[6] *The Civil War in France*, S.W., I, p. 474.

"the colossal productive forces developed within the capitalist system . . . are only waiting to be taken possession of by a society organised for co-operative working on a planned basis".[1]

So, again, he declares at the end of the first chapter of *Capital* that "the life-process of society, which is based on the process of material production, does not strip off its mystical veil until it is treated as production by freely associated men, and is consciously regulated by them in accordance with a settled plan".[2] We are told that the means of production will be held in common, and that the "settled plan" will "maintain the proper proportion between the different kinds of work to be done and the various wants of the community", so that the wants and the means of satisfying them will be so adjusted that the means will not be wasted or the wants remain unsatisfied. Yet this is nothing but utopianism. It assumes that everyone accepts the "plan"—an illusion fostered by the fiction that the proletariat is endowed with a homogeneous "class will". But even if the majority were to do so, what would be the position of the minority, which will have to be coerced? And as to the majority, who is to decide what the "various wants" are, and what priority is to be given to each?; and assuming that they vary with individuals, what criterion is to be adopted for satisfying them? It is clear that such matters can only be handled by some agency whose powers will then be incompatible with the existence of "freely associated men".[3] But Marx and Engels refuse to face this issue. They demand a planned society. But as to who is to do the planning, and upon what principles, they offer no guidance. As Lenin was later to complain, "Not a single book has been written about the state capitalism that exists under communism.

---

[1] p. 171.   [2] I, p. 51.
[3] J. A. Murray Macdonald, *Karl Marx and the Present Unrest*, 1920, pp. 35–39.

It did not even occur to Marx to write a word on the subject, and he died without leaving a single precise statement or irrefutable instruction on it. This is why we must get out of the difficulty entirely by our own efforts." [1]

Schlesinger has pointed out that Marx's criticism of the capitalist system is directed against its inadequacy rather than against the injustice of the distribution of the national income, upon which contemporary socialism lays such emphasis.[2] His system was egalitarian only in so far as it demanded the abolition of classes; for, as Engels put it, "any demand for equality which goes beyond that of necessity passes into absurdity".[3] Yet when Marx speaks of "the anarchy of social production", he is not simply objecting to its unorganised character. As we have seen, he distinguishes sharply between a primitive economy, in which the worker owns whatever he produces and is thus his own master, and a capitalist economy, in which he is enslaved by the products of his own labour; and it is this "fetishism of commodities" which is the cause of that alienation from which he suffers. The reason why there must be an economic transformation of society is at least as much to restore man to a true knowledge of himself by placing him once again in the right relation to production as it is to introduce order into production itself. Indeed, the latter implies the former. Hence it is necessary to abolish division of labour, since it is this which, according to Marx, "converts the product of labour into a commodity",[4] and with it the specialisation to which production under the capitalist system has led.

In the opening pages of his *Condition of the Working Class in England*, Engels describes the state of the weaver-cum-farmer under "social division of labour", in which he and his family do no more work than they chose and yet

---

[1] *Report to the Eleventh Congress*, March 1922, S.W., IX, p. 338.
[2] *Marx. His Time and Ours*, 1950, p. 354.
[3] *Anti-Dühring*, p. 123.   [4] *Capital*, I, p. 81.

produce all they require for their needs; and he shows how this idyllic mode of life changed under manufacture and machinofacture, until the day's work became reduced to the performance of what Marx calls "ossified particularisations". It may be noted in passing that if the picture Engels draws is a true one, what they both say elsewhere about division of labour as the cause throughout history of commodity production, classes, exploitation and the rest requires to be modified, as it would seem that it was not until the stage of manufacture that it became at all a serious evil. In his *Anti-Dühring*, however, Engels only tells us that "the former division of labour must disappear" and be replaced by an organisation which emancipates men "by giving each individual the opportunity to develop and exercise all his faculties, physical and mental in all directions, in which therefore productive labour will become a pleasure instead of a burden".[1] In their early years he and Marx had declared that, "In Communist society, where nobody has one exclusive sphere of activity but each can become accomplished in any branch he wishes, society regulates the general production, and thus makes it possible for me to do one thing today and another tomorrow, to hunt in the morning, fish in the afternoon, rear cattle in the evening, criticize after dinner, just as I have a mind, without ever becoming hunter, fisherman, shepherd or critic".[2] Nor did they revise this opinion. Thus Engels asserts that under socialism "there will no longer be any professional porters or architects, and the man who for half-an-hour gives instruction as an architect will also push a barrow for a period until his activity as an architect is once again required".[3] It may be that such expressions of opinion contain an element of fancy, but in writings in which there is so much that is extravagant it is hard to dis-

[1] *Capital*, I, pp. 328–329.
[2] *The German Ideology*, M.E.G.A., Abt. I, Bd. 5, p. 22; Eng. trans., p. 22.
[3] *Anti-Dühring*, pp. 228–229.

tinguish between what is to be taken seriously and what is not.

As for Marx, he indulges his bent for discovering economic laws to the point of representing the abolition of specialisation as one of them. "Modern industry . . . imposes the necessity of recognising as a fundamental law of production variations of work, consequently fitness of the labourer for varied work, consequently the greatest possible development of his varied aptitudes." [1] In the *Critique of the Gotha Programme* he speaks of the disappearance in the "higher phase of communist society" of "the enslaving subordination of the individual to division of labour"; [2] though if Engels is to be believed, we need not wait for communism to achieve this, since he tells us that "education allows young people quickly to familiarise themselves with all systems of production, and to alternate from one method to another depending on the needs of society".[3] But the problem of providing a variety of employments will presumably be facilitated by the abolition, which he assures us will take place under socialism, of the division between town and country, thus enabling industry and agriculture to exist side by side in the same area. He observes that there is nothing utopian about this, though he does not say how it is to be done, and it is singular that a man who had spent so much of his life as a Manchester industrialist should have shown no recognition of the difficulties involved.[4] According to Stalin, however, the division has now disappeared in the Soviet Union, though he adds that Engel's prediction that "the great towns will perish" has not been fulfilled.[5]

But it is in the *Critique of the Gotha Programme* that we come nearest to discovering what Marx believed that the future holds in store. He explains that after the revolution

---

[1] *Capital*, I, pp. 493–494. [2] S.W., II, p. 23.
[3] *Grundsätze des Kommunismus*, M.E.G.A., Abt. I, Bd. 6, p. 518.
[4] *The Housing Question*, S.W., I, p. 567.
[5] *Economic Problems of Socialism in the U.S.S.R.*, pp. 30–31.

there will be a transitional period during which men will be paid "according to their work", and not, as under communism, "according to their needs". But it will be temporary only: "In the higher phase of communist society, after the enslaving subordination of the individual under the division of labour has disappeared, and therewith the opposition between manual and intellectual labour; after labour has become not only a means of life, but also the highest want in life; when with the development of all the faculties of the individual, the productive forces have correspondingly increased, and all the springs of social wealth flow more abundantly—only then may the limited horizon of capitalist right be left behind, and society inscribe upon its banner: 'From each according to his faculties, to each according to his needs' ".[1] Hence there arose in socialist circles the belief that the proletarian revolution would be succeeded by two stages—the first, the probationary stage of socialism, and the second, the final stage of communism when men would have become emancipated from their enslavement to capitalist ideology.

Marx and Engels have a profound faith in the power of large-scale production, under capitalist technology, to bring about all they desire. It will educate the proletariat, though at best it can only develop technical efficiency (indeed not even that if what they say of the mechanical nature of labour under machinofacture holds good) [2] rather than those intellectual and moral qualities that will be called for if it is to take over production.[3] It will ensure abundance, as there will be no more crises and demand will be all the time effective, though in the *Critique of the Gotha Programme* the workers are warned that

---

[1] S.W., II, p. 23.

[2] Thus the *Communist Manifesto* declares that the worker is "an appendage of the machine, and it is only the most simple, most monotonous and most easily acquired knack that is required of him", S.W., I, p. 39.

[3] Walter Theiner, *Der Marxismus*, Berne, 1950, pp. 76–77.

even under socialism they will not receive the full value they create, as it will still be necessary to set aside a part of it for investment, replacements, social services and the like.[1] Above all, it will free them from alienation, as they will once again own what they produce, and will no longer suffer from the "idiotism" of specialisation. Yet there are no grounds for supposing that either will be so. It is true that under a primitive economy a man owns what he makes, and can exchange it with others like himself for the simple things which he requires and they produce. Under a highly developed industrial economy, which enables a vastly greater range of needs to be supplied, this is no longer possible; and the result will be, as Marx saw, to establish a new relation between the producer and the product. Marx assumes that this relation is an evil, and that it must lead to alienation which nothing short of the abolition of private enterprise will cure. But the transference of the means of production to society does not reverse the relation of the worker to the commodity he makes which remains just what it was before; and the only way to reverse it would be to get rid of industrial technology and return to a simpler mode of production, which, even if it were practicable, is the last thing Marx and Engels want to do. Nor is it possible to get rid of division of labour as long as the technology is retained, since men will still have to discharge the same functions whether their factory belongs to society or to the capitalist. Certainly the industrial development of the Soviet Union has led to an undreamt-of specialisation of the unskilled worker.

Lenin's views as to what a proletarian society should be are most fully set out in *The State and Revolution*, where their inspiration is the Commune. Developments after he had seized power soon compelled him to modify them, but they were not abandoned, and their realisation was

[1] S.W., II, p. 20.

simply postponed to the "higher phase" of communism. As he points out, proletarian democracy differs from bourgeois democracy in drawing the masses into active participation in the work of government, so that bureaucracy ceases to exist because everyone has become a bureaucrat. Again, it is not enough to expropriate the capitalists. The workers, organised into Co-operatives— once more on the model of the Commune—must take over and run production, which he believed, with extraordinary naivety, that capitalist technology had reduced to the simple operations of "accounting and control" which any literate worker who knew the four rules of arithmetic could perform.[1]

At the same time, Lenin had inherited the Marxist belief in planning as an essential feature of a socialist society,[2] and already before the revolution he had decided upon the framework within which it would take place. "Socialism", he declared, "is nothing but state capitalism which has been turned in the interest of the whole people and has therefore *ceased* to be a capitalist monopoly".[3] The disastrous failure of "workers' control of industry" strengthened this conviction, and in May 1918 he pointed out that "socialism is inconceivable without large-scale capitalist technique based upon the last word of modern science . . . without planned state organisation which subjects tens of millions of people to the strictest observance of a single standard of production and distribution". German state capitalism provided the model, so that all that was required was to substitute a proletarian state for the "junker-bourgeois imperialist

---

[1] S.W., VII, p. 42; cp. E. H. Carr, who points out that the notion of the simplicity of economic administration goes back to the nature school of the eighteenth century, "Lenin's Theory of the State" in *The Bolshevik Revolution*, 1950, I, p. 245, n. 1.

[2] Alexander Baykov makes this clear on the opening page of his *Development of the Soviet Economic System*, 1950.

[3] *The Impending Catastrophe and how to Combat It*, Sept. 1917, S.W., 2 vol., ed., II, p. 113.

state", and "we shall have the sum total of the necessary conditions for socialism". He went on to predict, with his accustomed optimism, that "if we introduce state capitalism in approximately six months time . . . within a year socialism will have gained a hold and have become invincible in our country".[1] Hence the programme adopted by the Eighth Congress in March 1919, in accordance with Lenin's directives, laid down as one of the primary tasks "the maximum unification of all the economic activities of the country in a comprehensive state plan".[2]

The writings of the last years of Lenin's life contain no further mention of the Commune. Yet he seems to have been conscious of the need to reconcile the centralised direction of economic planning by the state with the role which he had assigned to the proletarian dictatorship of the workers. In *The Food Tax* (April 1921) he declares, however, that the two are not incompatible, though he now returns to Engel's thesis that state capitalism is only the initial stage, as he goes on to speak of its transference into socialism "in the not too distant future".[3] But in the report he delivered to the Fourth Comintern Congress of November 1922 he maintains that in the Soviet Union state capitalism takes a "peculiar form", and one which differs from what is ordinarily understood by it, "in that the proletarian state not only owns the land, but also all the important sectors of industry".[4] State planning had clearly come to stay, but it could be justified on the assumption that under it the workers would grow in stature until they had "become accustomed to the performance of public duties without any specific machinery

---

[1] *Left-Wing Childishness and Petty-Bourgeois Mentality*, S.W., VIII, pp. 365–366.
[2] For Lenin's *Report to the Eighth Congress* see S.W., VIII, pp. 247 f. esp. pp. 258–259, 266–267.
[3] S.W., IX, p. 181.
[4] *Five Years of the Russian Revolution*, S.W., X, p. 329.

of compulsion, when unpaid work for the common good becomes the general phenomenon".[1]

To avoid misunderstanding it should be pointed out, however, that although planning was always accepted in principle and rudimentary attempts were made to practise it, it was many years before there was anything resembling what we understand by it today. According to Nicolas Timasheff, it was in 1919 that Lenin first became aware of its technical aspect through the writings of Walter Rathenau and the Russian professor V. I. Grinevetsy.[2] Yet although the State Planning Commission (Gosplan) was set up in 1921 as a commission of the Council of Labour and Defence, and with the strong support of Trotsky, who wished it to be given legislative powers, it was not until the first Five-Years Plan of 1928 that anything of a systematic nature took place, and even then much of the planning was based on trial and error, to judge by the results as officially reported.

The most complete description Stalin gives of what he calls "the anatomy of communist society" is in the statement he made on September 9, 1927, to the first American Labour Delegation, and it is of interest to note how closely it conforms with what has been set out above. "It is", he declares, "a society in which (a) there will be no private ownership of the means of production, but social, collective ownership; (b) there will be no classes or state but workers in industry or agriculture managing their economic affairs as a free association of toilers; (c) national economy, organised according to plan, will be based on the highest technique both in industry and agriculture; (d) there will be no antithesis between town and country, between industry and agriculture; (e) the products will be distributed according to the principle of

[1] "Subotniks, Report delivered to the Moscow City Conference of the B.K.P.(b)," Dec. 20, 1919, S.W., VIII, p. 239; cp. *The State and Revolution*, S.W., VII, p. 88.
[2] *The Great Retreat*, New York, 1941, p. 120.

the old French economists, 'From each according to his abilities, to each according to his needs'; (*f*) science and art will enjoy conditions conducive to their highest development; (*g*) the individual, freed from bread-and-butter cares, and from the necessity of cringing to the 'powerful of the earth', will become really free etc, etc". He concluded by observing that "clearly, we are still remote from such a society", and it would not appear that a quarter of a century has brought it much nearer.[1]

Stalin's statement in introducing the 1936 Constitution that the victory of socialism within the Soviet Union had been achieved, taken in conjunction with the extravagant claims made after the war that the country led the world in every field of activity, naturally aroused speculation as to when the Russian people, after close on forty years of wandering in the wilderness, would be entitled to enter the promised land. But in his *Economic Problems of Socialism in the U.S.S.R.*, he declared that "at least three preliminary conditions" must be satisfied. First, there must be a much higher level of production. Here he is simply following Lenin, who had laid down that "communism is the higher productivity of labour compared with capitalist productivity of labour, of establishing class-conscious united workers, employing advanced techniques".[2] Secondly, agriculture must be fully collectivised. In his *Dizzy with Success* (1930) he had admitted that it was not at the time desirable to advance beyond the artel;[3] but in his report to the Seventeenth Congress of 1934 he had made it clear that complete collectivisation was still the ultimate goal.[4] Thirdly, there must be such a general all-round improvement in the cultural standard as will enable all members of society "to be active agents of social development, and be in a position freely to

[1] *Leninism*, ed. 1933, II, pp. 70–71.
[2] *A Great Beginning*, June, 1919, S.W., IX, p. 432.
[3] *Leninism*, ed. 1933, II, p. 284.
[4] *ibid.*, ed. 1940, p. 506.

choose their occupations, and not be tied all their lives, owing to the existing division of labour, to some one occupation".[1] What he meant was that there must be a higher degree of technical efficiency, since for him culture and technology were identical.

Hence, Stalin's vision of the future is that of a collectivised society in which production has reached such a level as to make it possible to supply at least all the basic needs of its citizens. In the present stage, production has to be controlled, and Art. 11 of the 1936 Constitution provides for state-directed economic planning; but under communism society itself becomes responsible. As far as there is any theory behind this, it is that in time the masses will become so completely identified with the state as to render its continuance no longer necessary; but for any clear statement as to how this will be brought about we must go back to his address at the Sverdlov University of June 1925, in which he deals with the problem of how to bring them into the daily work of administration. He says, "It takes place through the mass initiative organisations, through commissions and committees of every conceivable kind. Around these committees . . . are teeming ant-hills of organisations that have sprung up of their own accord . . . comprising millions of non-party members, workers and peasants who, by their daily, inconspicuous, painstaking and silent efforts are building the foundations and creating the very life of the Soviets. . . . The Soviet state apparatus does not consist only of Soviets. In the fullest sense of the word, it consists of the Soviets and those non-party and party organisations which link up the Soviets with the very 'rank and file', which merge the state apparatus with the vast masses, and which, step by step, are *breaking down every semblance of a barrier between the state apparatus and the population*. This is how we must strive to increase the personnel of our state apparatus ten-fold,

[1] pp. 74–76.

merge it with the masses, and thus prepare the way for the transition to a stateless society, a communist society." [1]

What, then, we are left with is a society in which every activity is directed by a central agency, which needs pay no regard to the wishes of those it controls; and an assurance that one day this society will become one of free and equal men, no longer subject to coercion. Yet it will not do so until men have lost all trace of the acquisitive instinct and are prepared to work solely for the common good, and it is allegedly to assist this transformation that the Soviet citizen must be shielded from the maleficent influence of the outer world. But the assertion that human nature will undergo such a transformation is a genuflexion to mythology, and the condition upon which the emphasis has come increasingly to be laid is that there must first be a vast increase in productivity, to be achieved by raising the educational standard of the workers to that of the present technocracy, which constitutes the new middle class, and has inherited most of the traditions and prejudices of the class it has replaced. This differs, however, from the Marxist concept, according to which the proletariat was endowed with some mysterious virtue which entitled it to take over production, as it is the admission that there exists a class which is superior both in intelligence and capacity, and that the transition into communism depends upon the ability of the workers to raise themselves to its level.

[1] *Leninism*, ed. 1933, I, p. 299.

X

The Dictatorship of the Proletariat

"Revolutionary Marxism", that is, the doctrine which Marx and Engels taught and not its later emasculated form, makes three demands. First, that the bourgeois state must be destroyed. Secondly, that the means of production must be transferred to society with a view to setting up a rationally planned economy. Thirdly, that during the transition period between the abolition of capitalism and the establishment of communism the agency which will administer the new order will be a proletarian dictatorship. We have considered the first two of these demands, and must now turn to the third of them.

From the first, Marx and Engels wished to replace the bourgeois state by some other organisational form, though their early writings do not say what it is to be, and all we are told in the *Communist Manifesto* is that "in place of the old bourgeois society we shall have an association in which the free development of each is the condition for the free development of all". What would be the type of government in such an association is not stated, but it would not be political democracy, which Marx had rejected as early as 1844 in his *Critique of Hegel's Philosophy of Law*, where he describes it as "the religion" of social life, because it rests on an abstract view of man and opposes the purely formal functions assigned to him as a citizen to his real functions as a worker. Thus, as Roy Pascal says, Marx was already concerned with the problem of what sort of society would express the fact that the reality of man lies in his activity as a worker, and not in political activity; and he held that political democracy failed to produce such a society because it ignored man as he really is, and regarded his work—that is, the contribution he makes to society—as a matter of indifference.[1] He had intended to deal further with the matter in his commentary on those sections in which Hegel had discussed civil society, but that part of it was never written, and what he thought of the state as it ought to be has to be disengaged from his controversial writings inspired by particular events.

Of these events, by far the most important was the Paris Commune of 1871. Marx had been deeply impressed by it, for, as he told Kugelmann, it presented "a new point of departure of historic importance".[2] Engels indeed claimed that it had been based upon their own principles of "German scientific socialism"; [3] but in his *Civil War in France* Marx did not pretend that it had introduced any specifically socialist measures, and he told a correspondent some years later that it "was in no sense socialist, nor could it be".[4] At the same time he held that "its special measures could not but betoken the tendency of a government of the people by the people", that its intention was "the expropriation of the expropriators", and that its projected form of social organisation would have led to communism,[5] which Engels declares was "the exact opposite of Proudhon's doctrine", upon which that form had none the less been clearly modelled.[6]

Many years later Lenin was to point out that the Commune had been guilty of two errors. It had been carried away by "the Proudhonist illusion of establishing eternal justice in the country"—an admission of the very influence that Engels had been concerned to deny; and it had

---

[1] *Karl Marx: Political Foundations*, 1943, pp. 11–12.
[2] April 17, 1871, *Corresp.*, p. 311.
[3] *The Housing Question*, S.W., I, p. 554.
[4] Letter to Domela Nieuwenhuis, Feb. 22, 1881, *Corresp.*, p. 387.
[5] *The Civil War in France*, S.W., I, p. 474.
[6] Introduction to the 1891 German edition of *The Civil War in France*, S.W., I, p. 437.

shown "unnecessary magnanimity", since, "instead of annihilating its enemies, it had endeavoured to exercise moral influence over them".[1] He says that "Marx did not hide a single mistake of the Commune from the proletariat",[2] whereas in fact the only criticism the latter made at the time is contained in a letter to Kugelmann of April 12, 1871, where he points out that the leaders had committed an error in not marching on Versailles, and that the Central Committee of the National Guard had surrendered its powers too soon,[3] though he added later that the National Bank should have been seized, which Engels declared "would have been worth ten thousand hostages".[4] *The Civil War in France* does not refer to these shortcomings. None the less, the failure of the Commune led Marx and Engels to emphasise that the bourgeois state must be destroyed, and thus include in the preface to the 1872 edition of the *Communist Manifesto* the passage from *The Civil War* which laid down that "the working-class cannot simply lay hold of the ready-made state machine and wield it for their own purposes",[5] though according to Engels, the necessity for this had been recognised "from the very outset".[6]

Thereafter Marx and Engels regarded the Commune as prefiguring the future proletarian society. As Marx declares, "Its true secret was this. It was essentially a working class government, the product of the producing as against the appropriating class, the political form at last discovered under which to work out the emancipation of labour".[7] It was to be "a working, not a parliamentary body, legislative and executive at the same time".[8] Of the

---

[1] "Lessons of the Commune", *Zagranichnaya Gazeta*, March 23, 1908, reprinted in *The Paris Commune*, 1931, p. 17.
[2] Preface to the Russian edition of Marx's *Letters to Kugelmann*, Feb. 1907, S.W., II, p. 719.
[3] *Corresp.*, p. 309.   [4] *ibid.*, p. 387; S.W., I, p. 437.
[5] S.W., I, p. 468.   [6] S.W., I, p. 438.
[7] *The Civil War in France*, S.W., I, p. 473.
[8] *ibid.*, S.W., I, p. 471.

practical problems to which a government of this type would give rise they show no perception whatever. They never ask themselves how the supreme authority of the workers is to be reconciled with the powers which would have to be exercised by their leaders, who were merely their instruments, or how these powers would be controlled, seeing that there would no longer be that separation of the legislative and executive functions of government which serves to limit them. Their acceptance of the Commune as a viable form of government reveals a simplicity for which we must wait for Lenin's *State and Revolution* to find a parallel.[1]

The Civil War in France is the last of the polemical exercises in which Marx applied the economic interpretation of history to contemporary events. Its purpose was to demonstrate that, despite its failure, the Commune was the greatest achievement of which the proletariat had yet shown itself capable. But it was not until his *Critique of the Gotha Programme* of 1875 that he discussed in any detail the nature of the proletarian society. Here we meet again with the slogan of "the dictatorship of the proletariat" which he had hitherto used on only two occasions, the first being in his *Class Struggles in France*,[2] and the second in his letter to Weydemeyer of March 1852, in which he defined his contribution to the theory of the class struggle. He now lays down that "Between capitalist and communist society lies the transformation of the one into the other", and that in this transition period "the state can be nothing but *the revolutionary* dictatorship of the proletariat".[3] He explains that this does not represent the communist ideal, which belongs to the future. "What we have to deal with here is a communist society, not as it has *developed* on its own foundations, but, on the contrary,

---

[1] Abram L. Harris, "Utopian Elements in Marx's Thought", *Ethics*, Univ. of Chicago, Jan. 1950, pp. 93 f.
[2] S.W., I, p. 203.
[3] S.W., II, p. 30.

just as it emerges from capitalist society; which is thus, in every respect, economically, morally and intellectually, still stamped with the birthmarks of the old society from whose womb it is issuing".[1] Beyond this lies "the higher phase of communist society", which he describes in the celebrated passage quoted in the last chapter.

Thus Lenin was able to claim Marx's authority for the type of state which he set up after the October Revolution, and he bitterly attacked Kautsky for saying that the dictatorship was only a chance phrase (*Wörtchen*) to which Marx had attached no particular significance, pointing out that "Marx and Engels in their letters and in their published works *repeatedly* speak of it, especially both before and after the Commune".[2] Kautsky had argued further that when Marx had used the expression in the *Critique of the Gotha Programme* he was not thinking of "a form of government, but of a condition which arises when the proletariat has seized power".[3] Yet it is certain that Marx and Engels meant more by it than this. In *The Housing Problem* we are told that "every real proletarian party . . . has put forward a class policy, the organisation of the proletariat as an independent political party, as the primary condition of the struggle, and the dictatorship of the proletariat as its immediate aim".[4] Again, in an article attacking the "anti-authoritarians" who wanted the state to be "abolished at one stroke", he says, "Have these gentlemen ever seen a revolution? A revolution is the most authoritarian thing there is; it is the act whereby one part of the population imposes its will upon the other part by means of rifles, bayonets and cannon—authoritarian means, if such there be at all; and if the victorious party does not want to have fought in vain, it must maintain this rule by means of the terror which its arms inspire

[1] S.W., II, p. 21.
[2] *The Proletarian Revolution and the Renegade Kautsky*, S.W., VII, pp. 119-120.
[3] *The Dictatorship of the Proletariat*, Vienna, 1918, Eng. trans., 1920, p. 43.
[4] S.W., I, p. 556.

in the reactionaries. Would the Paris Commune have lasted a single day if it had not made use of this authority of the armed people? Should we not, on the contrary reproach it for not having used it freely enough?" [1]

Such opinions do not support Kautsky's thesis. Lenin was indeed guilty of a verbal inaccuracy. Yet, although Marx only uses the expression "dictatorship of the proletariat" on the three occasions noted above, both he and Engels frequently employ other forms of words which have much the same meaning. The dictatorship is indeed central to the Marxist doctrine, as it is the organ through which the reconstruction of society will be effected; and it was not without good reason that Lenin insisted that a Marxist is one who accepts it as an extension of the class struggle.[2]

How far, then, is the conception a democratic one? First, we have to note that, according to the *Communist Manifesto*, the proletarian movement differs from "all previous historic movements" in being "the self-conscious independent movement of the immense majority in the interests of the immense majority"; [3] and Engels re-asserts this in his *Anti-Dühring*, when he says that "the anarchy of production transforms the immense majority of men into proletarians", and that it is they who will ultimately put an end to the anarchy.[4] On the other hand, it must be borne in mind that it was essential to Marx's analysis of the decline of capitalism that the proletariat *should* become the vast majority; and that when he had to deal with a concrete revolutionary situation, as in the case of the Commune, he was entirely indifferent to the fact that it did not constitute a majority in France or in any other European country, as Lenin himself admitted.[5] Certainly Engels had no illusions as to what the position

[1] *On Authority*, Feb. 1873, S.W., I, p. 578.
[2] *The State and Revolution*, S.W., VII, p. 33.
[3] S.W., I, p. 42. [4] p. 307.
[5] *The State and Revolution*, S.W., VII, p. 33.

was likely to be in the day of revolution; for, as he told Bebel, "Whenever the bourgeoisie feel seriously threatened, they will always ally themselves with the most radical bourgeois party, and will be supported by the petty bourgeoisie and the rural population", so that "it cannot be expected that at the moment of crisis we shall have the majority of the electorate, and therefore of the nation, behind us".[1]

That Engels occasionally uses language which suggests a contrary opinion is attributable to the aversion which he and Marx came to entertain for Blanquism in the sense of "putschism". In an article written in 1874, when they were trying to hold in check the disintegrating influence of the Communard exiles, he points out that the revolution must be the work of the whole revolutionary class, and not the *coup de main* of a minority, and that Blanquism would lead to "the dictatorship of a small number, that is, of those who have carried out the *coup de main*, but were themselves subject to the dictatorship of one or more persons".[2] So again, in his introduction to the 1895 edition of Marx's *Class Struggles in France* he declares that "the time of surprise attacks, of revolutions carried through by small conscious minorities at the head of unconscious masses, is past. When it is a question of the complete transformation of the social organisation, the masses themselves must be in it, must themselves already have grasped what is at stake, what they are going in for body and soul. The history of the last fifty years has taught us that."[3]

Yet all this is perfectly consistent with a revolution carried out by a proletarian minority which claims to be supported by the "toiling masses"—the *modus operandi* that Lenin was to employ. For he, too, professed to reject

[1] Dec. 11, 1884, *Corresp.*, p. 443.
[2] "Programme of the Blanquist Refugees of the Commune", *Volkstaat*, No. 7, 1874, quoted by Leo Figuères, *Cahiers du Communisme*, April 1953.
[3] S.W., I, p. 123.

Blanquism, which had become discredited by the close of the century as the expression of socialism's immaturity; and it is significant that when he appealed to Marx's authority in support of the dictatorship of the proletariat he did not make use of the passage in the *Class Struggles in France*, where it is mentioned in connection with that "revolutionary socialism . . . for which the bourgeoisie has itself invented the name of Blanqui".[1] As he declared, "In order to obtain state power, the class-conscious workers must win the majority to their side. . . . We are not Blanquists. We are not in favour of seizure of power by a minority".[2] But he does not say that the workers must themselves constitute a majority. On the contrary, he contends that, "in times of revolution it is not sufficient to ascertain the 'will of the majority'; that at the decisive moment one must *prove to be the stronger* . . . one must *be victorious*", and he goes on to explain that "in all the large-scale revolutionary movements . . . up to 1905, we see innumerable examples of how the more organised, more class-conscious, better armed minority forces its will upon the majority and is victorious over it".[3]

Similarly, when he was faced in December 1917 with the problem of the Constituent Assembly, which was due to meet in the following month, he argued that "to consider the question from a formal, legal point of view, within the limits of ordinary bourgeois democracy and ignoring the class struggle and civil war, would be a betrayal of the cause of the proletariat".[4] This might be discounted as polemics, since his immediate objection to the Assembly was that his own party was in a minority. But in an article written early in 1920 he states the position in more general terms: "The traitors, blockheads, and pedants of the Second International could never

[1] S.W., I, p. 203.
[2] *A Dual Power*, April 1917, S.W., VI, p. 29.
[3] *On Constitutional Illusions*, Aug. 1917, S.W., VI, p. 182.
[4] *Theses on the Constituent Assembly*, Dec. 1917, S.W., VI, pp. 450–451.

145

understand this dialectics—that the proletariat cannot triumph unless it wins a majority of the population over to its side—and that to confine the winning of a majority to, or make it conditional upon, obtaining a majority of votes at the polls under the rule of the bourgeoisie is either the densest stupidity, or a sheer attempt to fool the workers". He then explains that "in order to win over the majority of the population", the proletariat must first seize power, smash the old state apparatus and then complete the destruction of its bourgeois and petty bourgeois opponents.[1] This is an interesting theory. The revolution is not the act of the majority, since it is only *after* it has taken place that the majority is won over. The dictatorship is not therefore a dictatorship of the majority. "It is", as he says, "a dictatorship of the revolutionary people, not of the whole people." [2]

Yet even if the proletariat were to constitute a majority, it would not be justified in liquidating the bourgeoisie—and of course the petty bourgeoisie with it. But to do so is its primary objective, to which it is committed by the doctrine of the class struggle. For in Marx's theory the proletariat is the nation, just as Jacobin theory identified "the people" with it. The bourgeoisie is the class enemy whose sectional interests are opposed to those of the masses, and therefore to the common good of society. It does not belong to the nation, and will have no part or lot in the new order.[3] Yet it may be observed that when the bourgeoisie became the dominant class, it did not destroy the "feudal lords" whom it had replaced. As a class they were greatly enriched by the development of capitalism,

---

[1] *The Elections to the Constituent Assembly*, Dec. 1919, S.W., VI, p. 475. cp. *The Proletarian Revolution and the Renegade Kautsky*: "To assume that in a revolution . . . the issue is decided simply by the relation between the majority and the minority is the acme of stupidity, the stupid prejudice of a common or garden liberal, the deception of the masses". S.W., VII, p. 140.
[2] *History of the Question of the Dictatorship*, Oct. 1920, S.W., VII, p. 254.
[3] Talmon, *op. cit.*, pp. 74–75, 94–95.

to which many of them contributed; and although in England their political power was curtailed by electoral reforms and the acceptance of the principle of the ascendancy of the Lower House, they remained exceedingly influential, and the more successful members of the new class intermarried with them, and adopted their standard of values and mode of life.

Secondly, in his criticism of the Erfurt Programme of 1891 Engels declares that, "If anything is certain, it is that our own party can only come to power under the form of a democratic republic. Precisely this is the scientific form of the dictatorship of the proletariat, as the great French Revolution (he means, of course, the Commune) has already shown"; [1] and in his preface to the 1891 edition of Marx's *Civil War in France* it is with the Commune that the dictatorship is once again identified. "Well and good, gentlemen; do you want to know what the dictatorship looks like? Look at the Paris Commune. That was the dictatorship of the proletariat." [2]

The first of these statements is frequently quoted as evidence of Engels' democratic sympathies. But this rests upon a misapprehension. In his *Eighteenth Brumaire* Marx had laid down that the bourgeois republic "signifies *in general only the political form of revolution of bourgeois society* and not its *conservative form of life*"; [3] while in the *Critique of the Gotha Programme* he had referred to that "vulgar democracy which sees the millennium in the democratic republic, and has no conception that it is precisely in this last form of state of bourgeois society that the class struggle has to be fought to its conclusion". [4] Thus Engels tells Bernstein that "the first and immediate result of the revolution, as far as its form is concerned, cannot be any other than the bourgeois republic", and that it is this that will

---

[1] *Corresp.*, p. 486; Engels' criticism of the Programme was published in *Neue Zeit*, 1901–1902, pp. 5–13.
[2] S.W., I, p. 440.   [3] S.W., I, p. 232.   [4] S.W., II, p. 31.

"render it possible to win over the great mass of the workers to socialism":[1] for, as he points out, "the democratic revolution always remains the last form of bourgeois domination, that in which it is broken to pieces" (*die in der es kaput geht*).[2] Lenin was to make the same point in *The State and Revolution* when he declared that "a democratic republic is the best possible political shell for capitalism", his meaning being that it enabled "the omnipotence of wealth" to entrench itself behind a façade of pseudo-democratic institutions.[3] It is therefore clear that Engels' reference to it in connection with the Erfurt Programme was made in no complimentary sense, and that he simply meant, as he had explained in his *Origin of the Family*, that it was "the highest form of state which, under our modern conditions of society, is becoming more and more inevitable, the form of state in which the last decisive struggle between the bourgeoisie and the proletariat can be fought out".[4]

Further, it must be remembered that, according to the Marxist theory of revolution as applied to a society which still contained feudal elements, the role of the bourgeoisie (or of the petty bourgeoisie if the bourgeoisie fail to rise to the occasion) is to prepare the way for a proletarian revolution; and thus at the time of the 1848 revolutions Marx opposed an extremist group in Cologne which advocated a complete breach with it in favour of the policy of assisting it to come into power, and then using it to obtain such reforms as would gradually strengthen the proletariat until it was able to seize power for itself. The position is stated lucidly, if not altogether tactfully, in an article which Engels contributed to the *Deutsch-Brusseler Zeitung* of January 23, 1848: "Fight on bravely then, gentlemen of capital. We need your help: we need even

---

[1] Aug. 27, 1883, *Briefe von F. Engels an E. Bernstein*, pp. 129–130.
[2] Mar. 24, 1884, *ibid.*, I, p. 142.
[3] S.W., VII, p. 15.   [4] S.W., II, p. 291.

your rule upon occasions. For it is you who must clear from our path the relics of the Middle Ages and of absolute monarchy. You must abolish monarchy, you must centralise, you must change the more or less destitute classes into real proletarians—recruits for us. It is your factories and trade connections that must lay the foundations for the liberation of the proletariat. Your reward shall be a brief period of rule. You shall dictate laws, and bask in the sun of your own majesty. But remember—the hangman's foot is upon the threshold."[1]

Thirdly, the introduction of universal suffrage into Germany in 1866, and the extensions of the suffrage in England in 1867 and 1884 might well have led Marx and Engels to revise their doctrine. When they wrote the *Communist Manifesto* there was much truth in the contention that "the worker has no country". Now a new situation was arising. In the preface to the 1872 edition of the *Manifesto* they declare that the passage at the end of Section II, dealing with revolutionary measures, "would in many respects be written differently today", as it had "in some details become antiquated".[2] Yet it was not until the last year of his life that Engels took stock of the position in the introduction to the German edition of Marx's *Class Struggles in France*, and even then what he says has to be looked at twice. For the introduction is dated March 6, 1895, and from January to April of that year a Reichstag committee was considering a measure (the so-called *Umsturzvorlage*) designed to tighten existing legislation against socialist propaganda. As Engels told Kautsky, he had felt it necessary to take the apprehensions of "our Berlin friends" into account; and, in commenting on Engels' letter, Kautsky adds, "It is clear that in view of the situation Engels avoided anything which could be used by its enemies against the party, and that thus, while naturally

---

[1] M.E.G.A., Abt. I, Bd. 6, pp. 397–398.
[2] S.W., I, pp. 21–22.

holding fast to essentials, he expressed himself as moderately as he could." [1]

In this introduction Engels admits that he and Marx had misjudged the situation in 1848, as the time had not yet come for the elimination of capitalist production. "History has proved us, and all who thought like us, wrong." With the failure of the Commune the centre of gravity of the European workers' movement had shifted to Germany, as Marx had foretold, and in consequence of universal suffrage the Social-Democratic Party had grown rapidly. He pointed out that while the French party, in the programme adopted in 1880, had accepted the suffrage as an instrument of emancipation, the Latin countries had long regarded it as a snare, although the *Communist Manifesto* had declared that "the winning of universal suffrage to be one of the most important tasks of the militant proletariat". But it was above all in Germany that it had proved its value. "We can count today on two and a quarter million votes. If it continues in this fashion, by the end of the century we shall conquer the great part of the middle strata of society, petty-bourgeois and small peasants, and grow into the decisive power in the land before which all other powers will have to bow whether they like it or not. We, the 'revolutionaries', are thriving far better on legal than on illegal methods." [2]

Yet there is no indication that Engels regarded the suffrage as anything more than a device for seizing power. As he tells Bernstein, "In my opinion, what should be

---

[1] Karl Diehl, *Über Sozialismus, Kommunismus und Anarchismus*, Jena, 1922, p. 145. For the Introduction see S.W., I, pp. 109–127. It first appeared, with certain excisions, in *Vorwärts* and *Neue Zeit*, and in letters to Kautsky and Lafargue of April 1 and 3, 1895, Engels complained that the text had been tampered with. It was not until after the October Revolution that it was published in full from his manuscript, and this is given in the *Selected Works*. The French edition of *Les Luttes des Classes* (Éditions Sociales, 1946), prints the omitted passages in square brackets (see Ch-F Hubert, "Initiation bibliographique à l'oeuvre de Marx et d'Engels", in H. C. Desroche's *Signification du Marxisme*, Paris, 1948, p. 334).

[2] S.W., I, pp. 124–125.

said is this: the proletariat too requires democratic forms for the seizure of political power, but like all political forms, they serve it only as a means".[1] Once it is in power, it will set up its dictatorship as the expression of its class will, and when Lenin said that this rested upon "power won and maintained by the violence of the proletariat against the bourgeoisie, power that is unrestricted by any laws", he was only expressing the views of Marx and Engels in somewhat more forcible language.[2]

As to whether the imposition of the dictatorship must involve a revolution in the sense of a popular rising, Marx and Engels do not absolutely commit themselves. The transition from quantity into quality does not necessarily imply violence. Yet Bober is right in maintaining that in their early writings it is towards violent revolution that the balance is inclined, as they hold (a) that the ruling class will never submit without a struggle, (b) that the building of communism by the workers calls for qualities which are most likely to be brought out in the fires of revolution, and (c) that a revolution will accelerate the transition from capitalism into socialism.[3] Thus Engels tells Marx in 1846 that he has been explaining to the German workers in Paris that communism means the achieving of the interests of the proletariat through the abolition of private property, and that they should "recognise no means of carrying out these objects other than a revolution by force".[4] According to the *Communist Manifesto*, "the Communists openly declare that their ends can be attained only by the forcible overthrow of all existing institutions". *The Poverty of Philosophy* ends on the same note with a distich of George Sand's, "Combat or death; bloody struggle or extinction; it is thus that the question is inevitably posed".

[1] March 24, 1884, *Briefe von F. Engels an E. Bernstein*, p. 142.
[2] *The Proletarian Revolution and the Renegade Kautsky*, S.W., VII, p. 123.
[3] *op. cit.*, pp. 262–263.
[4] Oct. 23, 1846. *Corresp.*, p. 2; see Lenin's comment on this, *The Marx-Engels Correspondence*, March 1913, S.W., II, pp. 46–47.

It is sometimes alleged that in his later years Marx ceased to approve of violence, but in view of his glorification of the Commune, it would be as well not to be too dogmatic about this. In an article of 1867 he says, "As for the social revolution, what does this word mean if not the class struggle. It is possible that the struggle between the workers and the capitalists will be less fierce and bloody than that between the feudal lords and the capitalists in England and France. Let us hope so."[1] But the statement most frequently quoted as evidence of a change of heart is that which he made in his address to the Amsterdam section of the First International of September 8, 1872. "We know that the institutions and customs of the various countries must be considered, and we do not deny that there are countries like England and America, and if I understood your arrangements better, I might even add Holland, where the worker may attain his object by peaceful means". Yet he went on to say, "Even so, we have to recognise that in *most continental countries* force will have to be the lever of the revolution. *It is to force that in due time the worker will have to appeal* if the domination of labour is at long last to be established".[2]

India was presumably another country where this would be necessary, and in 1882 Engels, who expected a revolution to break out there, told Kautsky with seeming complacency that "it will not pass off without all sorts of destruction, of course, but that sort of thing is inseparable from all revolutions".[3] Yet although Lenin never pretended that it was possible to seize power without a revo-

---

[1] *Poland's European Mission* printed by Paul W. Blackstock and Bert F. Hoselitz in *The Russian Menace to Europe*, pp. 107–108.

[2] G. M. Stekloff, *History of the First International*, Eng. trans., 1928, pp. 240–241. It is hard to believe that Marx was altogether sincere in making the above exceptions. He had no real knowledge of American conditions, while the state of the working-class movement in England gave him no cause for satisfaction, and he had sharply criticised its leaders at the recently concluded Hague Congress (see Stekloff, pp. 221 f., and Marx to Kugelmann, May 18, 1874, in *Marx–Engels on Britain*, p. 509).

[3] Sept. 12, 1882, *Corresp.*, p. 399.

lution, he too, upon occasions, deprecated violence. "The Jacobins of the twentieth century will not guillotine the capitalists; following a good example does not necessarily mean imitating it. It would be sufficient to arrest fifty of a hundred magnates and bank leaders." [1] That this is all that will be necessary is an illusion common to revolutionaries. At the same time, Lenin changes his tune in *The State and Revolution*, and declares that "the systematic repression of the exploiting minority calls for the greatest ferocity and savagery", though even so he contends that "no special apparatus of repression is needed" as it "will be done by the armed people itself, as simply and as readily as any crowd of civilised people . . . parts two people who are fighting". [2]

It is in *The State and Revolution* that Lenin elaborates the conception of the dictatorship of the proletariat which he had taken over from Marx. The transformation of the proletariat into the ruling class is, he insists, identical with democracy. As, however, democracy is a form of state, it is destined to disappear, but it is essential that the state be retained in the period following the revolution. He then argues that democracy can only exist under socialism because, under any other economy, there will always be a dominant class which manipulates the government in its own interests. Under capitalism therefore democracy is "only for the rich", whereas "proletarian democracy" is "true democracy", the "most complete democracy" and "a million times more democratic than any bourgeois state". [3] For he maintains that "the mechanism of capitalist democracy" reveals restrictions everywhere—residential qualifications for suffrage, the exclusion of women, obstacles to the right of assembly ("public buildings are not for beggars"), the capitalist organisation of the press, etc.—and that their effect is to "exclude

[1] *Pravda*, June 20, 1917, *Coll. Works*, XX, Bk. II, p. 220.
[2] S.W., VII, pp. 82–83.   [3] S.W., VII, pp. 78–81.

and squeeze out the poor from politics, from taking an active part in democracy".[1] These statements, as Hans Kelsen says, are either in open contradiction with the facts or are gross exaggerations; and in fact Lenin himself rejects them by contending that the rights conceded under bourgeois democracy are of great importance to the proletariat in its struggle against the capitalists, which is meaningless if they exist only for the rich.[2]

Moreover, Lenin argues that the dictatorship of the proletariat is itself obliged to impose "a series of restrictions on the freedom of the oppressors", and that "it is clear that where there is suppression, there is also violence, there is no freedom, no democracy"; and in *The Proletarian Revolution and the Renegade Kautsky* he admits that the soviet form is not "true democracy" because a whole class has been disenfranchised. Whether "the impending revolution in Europe" will be accompanied by a similar restriction he cannot say. But it is not necessarily implied in the idea of the dictatorship. What is essential to that idea is "the forcible suppression of the exploiters as a class . . . that is, of equality and freedom in respect of that class",[3] his meaning being that the bourgeoisie need not be disenfranchised if it can be crushed without it. His conclusion is therefore that "true democracy" is only possible under socialism, that is, when all resistance has been crushed and the classless society has been established. As, however, the state will then disappear, and democracy as a form of state with it, this means that there will only be democracy when democracy no longer exists. For, as he himself puts it, "While the state exists there is no freedom. When freedom exists there is no state."[4] But all these "absurd contradictions", as Kelsen calls them, are the inevitable consequence of the fact that the dictator-

[1] S.W., VII, p. 80.
[2] *The Political Theory of Bolshevism*, University of California Press, 1949, pp. 49 f.   [3] S.W., VII, p. 183.
[4] *The State and Revolution*, S.W., VII, p. 87.

ship of the proletariat was not a democracy, though it had to be represented as such because the Bolshevik leaders, including Lenin, had intended that the regime which would set up after the revolution should be a democratic one.

The truth is that the conception of the dictatorship is not a "democratic" one unless "democracy" is to be interpreted in the Jacobin sense, that is, as the rising of the people who by their very act abrogate all law and impose their "common will", which soon turns out to be that of their leaders. For, as Robert A. Dahl points out, democracy rests on the assumption that there are bound to be conflicts of interests within society, that these conflicts should be decided by the will of the majority, that minorities have the right to convert themselves into majorities by constitutional means, and that it is therefore necessary that political parties be formed in order to ascertain what the will of the majority is and give effect to it.[1] Lenin had not originally intended to suppress the rival Menshevik and Social Revolutionary parties; but the momentum of the revolution not only led him to do so, but also eventually to forbid the formation of any "fractions" within his own, thus establishing the "one-party" system which has ever since continued. Yet all this was written into Marx's doctrine of the dictatorship. For what is to happen to the bourgeoisie after the revolution, or indeed to any other group which it may be decided to regard as counter-revolutionary? They will be deprived of economic power, and presumably of political power also, since it is inconceivable that Marx, who would go to any lengths to crush a socialist opponent, would have permitted their members to organise themselves politically to defeat the objects for which the revolution had been carried out. The very notion of the "withering away" of

[1] "Marxism and Free Parties", *Review of Politics*, Nov. 1948, pp. 787 f.

the state is incompatible with parliamentary democracy, which he had already condemned on other grounds. The dictatorship belongs, in fact, to the Jacobin tradition. There is only one class will, and it will be realised in a classless society. In such a society there can be no room for more than one party, for if other parties agree with it they are superfluous, while if they do not, they are counter-revolutionary.

Bertram Wolfe holds that Lenin was a democrat up to 1917, and that his abandonment of democracy after the October Revolution was "the tragic climax of his career".[1] His conception of the party as a "narrow party" of professional revolutionaries rather than as a democratic labour movement is indeed often represented as a breach with the Marxist libertarian theory, and as having prepared the way for Stalinism.[2] None the less, it has a good Marxist paternity. Schlesinger has pointed to the resemblance between the Communist League after it had been reorganised by Marx and Engels and Lenin's notion of what a party should be as set out in his *One Step Forward, Two Steps Back*, and he contends that the League was a communist party in the modern sense of the word.[3] It was a secret society with a territorial organisation and a central apparatus similar to that of any such party today, and, as Engels later declared, it proved in its short lifetime "an excellent school for revolutionary activity".[4] Its statutes obliged all members to give proof of "faith in communism", practise "a revolutionary zeal in propaganda", and abstain from joining any "anti-communist"

---

[1] *Three who made a Revolution*, New York, 1948, p. 588.
[2] See G. L. Arnold, "Stalinism", *Political Quarterly*, 1950, pp. 338 f. and esp. p. 341.
[3] *op. cit.*, pp. 268–269; see Arthur Crispien, "Der Einfluss des marxistischen Ideen auf der internationale Arbeiterbewegung" in *Marx der Denker und Kämpfer*, Berlin, 1933, p. 56, and Otto Kuusinen, *The Communist Manifesto. A Programmatic Document of the Dictatorship of the Proletariat*, New York, Feb. 1934, p. 198.
[4] *On the History of the Communist League* (1885), S.W., II, p. 318.

political or national movement; while it was laid down that "whoever does not conform to these conditions will be expelled".[1]

It is true that the *Communist Manifesto* declares that the communists "do not form a separate party opposed to other working class parties". Yet they are the active, militant and class-conscious element of the working class, "its most advanced and resolute section . . . which pushes forward all others, and has the advantage over the working masses "of clearly understanding . . . the conditions and ultimate general results of the proletarian movement".[2] As Carl Friedrich has observed, the conception of an élite is part and parcel of the Marxist doctrine of the class struggle, which assumes that in every class there will be men of unusual insight who understand the laws which govern society, and have the will to use their knowledge.[3] After the failure of the 1848 revolutions, Marx recognised that there was no immediate prospect of a revolution, and at the meeting of the Central Committee of the Communist League September 15, 1850, which led to its dissolution, he completely reversed the revolutionary line he had advocated six months earlier, and declared that "the workers must go through fifteen, twenty perhaps even fifty years of war and civil war not only to alter existing conditions, but to make themselves fit to take over political power".[4] Conditions after 1848 called in fact for a mass party, and to these the heterogeneous composition of the First International similarly corre-

---

[1] M.E.G.A., Abt. I, Bd. 6, pp. 641–645.
[2] S.W., I, p. 44. In a letter to Kautsky of Aug. 12, 1892 Engels complains that Hyndman's Social Democratic Federation "has ossified Marxism into a dogma and, by rejecting *every* labour movement which is not orthodox Marxism . . . that is, by pursuing the exact opposite of the policy recommended in the *Manifesto*, it renders itself incapable of ever becoming anything else but a sect" (*Marx–Engels on Britain*, p. 528). This criticism would carry greater weight if he and Marx had not made a dead set against Hyndman and his movement, largely on personal grounds.
[3] *The New Belief in the Common Man*, New York, 1945, pp. 245–246.
[4] Franz Mehring, *Karl Marx*, ed. 1948, p. 206.

sponded. Yet Marx did not regard such a party as capable of carrying out a revolution, for as he told Bolte in 1871, as long as "sects" exist within a workers' organisation "the working class is not ripe for an independent historic movement", for "as soon as it attains maturity, all sects are essentially reactionary". He went on to point out that the history of the First International had been a continual struggle on the part of the General Committee, over which he had presided, "against the sects and amateur experiments which tried to maintain their position . . . against the real interests of the working class", that is, against what he held those interests to be.[1]

How far Marx ever seriously believed that the workers were capable of spontaneously generating a revolution is debatable. Lenin had the advantage of having been able to observe the transition of revolutionary Marxism into reformism, and the conclusion he drew from this was that the workers, if left to themselves, would never advance beyond "trade union consciousness",[2] and that a revolution must be carried out by an élite, albeit one which, unlike the Blanquist variety, was in close contact with the masses. That the October Revolution has led to so much misery makes it indeed permissible to regret that it ever took place at all. Yet unless we are to condemn revolutions as such, it is not easy to see upon what principle we are to blame Lenin for carrying out his own, and for using those means which alone enabled him to do so successfully. To have achieved it through a broadly-based democratic party would have been impossible, and indeed he had difficulty enough in persuading many of his closest associates to go through with it. It was inevitable that his revolutionary party should have become the nucleus of the new governmental apparatus; and in view of his uncom-

[1] Nov. 23, 1871, *Corresp.*, p. 315.
[2] For his attack on "spontaneity" see *What is to be done?*, S.W., II, pp. 51–65 and especially pp. 53 and 61.

promising temperament, it was equally inevitable that, having seized power, he should have refused to share it with the Mensheviks and Social Revolutionaries, though from at least 1921 they would have been prepared to have collaborated with him. Bertrand Russell has observed that no man can be a great reformer without having a larger belief in the value of his own judgement than reason warrants, and if Lenin had not possessed it in an uncommon degree, there would have been no revolution. It is not to be expected that a man who, after years of revolutionary agitation, had at last gained his desire, should be prepared peaceably to discuss alternative policies with those whom he regarded as his political opponents, and this in a country where such democratic procedures were unknown.

Had Lenin set up a liberal regime in Russia, his revolution would long ago have been forgiven him. But the principles by which he was inspired, and the circumstances under which they were applied, made this impossible. Thus, as we have seen, a contradiction arose, which time was to render increasingly acute, since it became necessary to argue that the dictatorship of the proletariat which, despite Stalin's disclaimers, never was, nor indeed could be, anything more than the dictatorship of the party *over* the proletariat, expressed the will of the masses, though as early as 1921 the Kronstadt mutiny had proved that it did not, as Lenin himself admitted at the Tenth Congress of that year.[1] Yet for all that he has to say about its central importance, the term has almost completely disappeared from the communist vocabulary, and in the revised Party Statutes of 1952 it has been deleted from those articles in which it was formerly used.[2] It is significant that the Chinese

[1] See the stenographic report of the Proceedings published by the Marx–Engels–Lenin Institute in 1933, p. 382.
[2] David J. Dallin, "The New Soviet Intelligentsia", *Yale Review*, Winter, 1953, pp. 193–194.

Communist Party leaders have avoided it, and have preferred the expression "hegemony of the proletariat".

At the time of the Commune Marx observed to Kugelmann that "world history would indeed be easy to make if the struggle were taken up only in conditions of infallibly favourable circumstances".[1] In October 1917 Lenin gambled on a revolution in the West, and the fact that it did not occur changed the whole situation, as the new Soviet state was left to fend for itself in a hostile world. Marx had declared that "law can never be higher than the economic structure of cultural development of society"; and as Plamenatz points out, this means in plain English that it is impossible to bring about a genuine socialist revolution except in a highly developed country.[2] The attempt by a party to impose socialist institutions upon a backward people is bound to lead to a dictatorship, under which the national interests will be subordinated to the determination of the leadership to retain power; while if any single leader proves strong enough, the system will end in his personal domination. Since the disappearance of Stalin various steps have been taken to preserve the regime. The principle of "one man leadership" has been disavowed in favour of that of "collective leadership"; more consumer goods have been promised; greater freedom of criticism has been permitted; and it may even be that since the fiasco of the "doctors' plot" and the fall of Beria the secret police has been subjected to some measure of control. Whether such steps will be effective it is still too early to say. Certainly they do not imply any disposition to revise the doctrine upon which the supremacy of the party rests.

The fiction that the Soviet Union is a proletarian democracy continues therefore to be maintained, and although in a speech of November 6, 1941, Stalin declared

[1] April 17, 1871, *Corresp.*, p. 310.
[2] "Deviations from Marxism", *Political Quarterly*, Jan.–March 1950, p. 53.

that England and the United States were democratic countries, despite their capitalist economies, the old arguments are once again used to represent that western democracy is fraudulent as possessing the form without the content. As Vyshinsky puts it, "In bourgeois society, based upon the principle of private property, the dictatorship of capital is complete in all spheres of life. . . . All the privileges and political freedoms are confirmed on behalf of the dominant class, and all the obligations are foisted on to the shoulders of the exploited." [1] "Only the victory of the socialist revolution made true political freedom and equality of civil rights possible", by establishing proletarian democracy, of which the Stalinist Constitution is "the highest expression". He admits that no society is democratic in which the citizens do not possess the four freedoms—of conscience, speech, the press and of association. Under the Soviet conception of the first, "the individual has the right to observe any religion" or "to follow no religion" and "to practise anti-religious propaganda"; but the right to engage in "religious propaganda" is not conceded, and "religious fanaticism" is punishable by law. As for the other freedoms, the workers possess them, but not the non-labouring strata, who are not to be allowed "to poison the minds of the masses and introduce confusion into their consciousness". To the rest of the population, however, they are "fully guaranteed", subject to "the single condition that they are utilised in accordance with the interests of the toilers and for the purpose of strengthening the socialist social order". As to whether they are so utilised, the party is the sole judge.[2]

In the contention that western democracy is formal only there is naturally at times an element of truth, seeing that no political system has yet been devised which the ingenuity of man cannot pervert. The liberal democratic

[1] *The Law of the Soviet State*, 1948, p. 546.
[2] *ibid.*, pp. 615–617.

tradition has indeed been challenged by Berdyaev in a number of writings upon the grounds that it is individualist in principle, and offers no guarantee of the freedom of personality, which, he holds, can be realised only within a Christian community.[1] But the communists have other reasons for rejecting it, though as they are sensitive to the charge of being "undemocratic", they have been careful to retain its outward form. Yet the result has only been to accentuate the divergence. According to western ideas, the people have the right to decide how they will be governed. Elections are held for this purpose, and they are not invalidated by the fact that pressure groups may seek to sway the decision in a given direction, as there will always be others which exert a contrary influence. But, according to the communists, the formal machinery of democracy—"free elections and the like—offers no guarantee that the government appointed will pursue a genuinely "democratic" policy. Hence they hold that the party, as the vanguard, must impose a "democratic" order—identified in their minds with a socialist revolution—and having thus provided the requisite conditions, hold elections under such circumstances as will ensure that the masses approve what has been done in their name.

This attitude was exemplified in the exchanges between the Soviet Government and the Western Powers which took place in 1952, and in particular by the Soviet Note of August 23, 1952. The Soviet Government was pressing at the time for the convening of a Four-Power conference on Germany. The Western Powers had agreed to this, but had made clear, as they have continued to do, that the agenda must be to decide how free elections should be conducted, on the basis of which a United German Government would be set up with which a peace treaty could then be negotiated. The Soviet

[1] For a summary of his views see Evgueny Lampert, *Nicolas Berdyaev and the New Middle Ages*, n.d., pp. 84 f.

Note reversed this order. The conference must first deal with the preparation of a peace treaty, next with the establishment of a central government, and last with the question of elections. To the western mind this suggests the procedure of "Sentence first, verdict afterwards". It is in fact entirely consistent with the Soviet concept of democracy.[1]

This concept all communists accept. Yet it would be a mistake to conclude that the system of government to which it has given rise in Russia is unchangeable. If our thesis is correct, that system is implicit in Marx's teaching, and is one that the October Revolution rendered inevitable, so that the question as to whether it might be less oppressive than it is is scarcely worth discussing, as it it no more than one of degree. Yet even under Stalin, its form was influenced by the impact of western ideas; and for all its crudity, the 1936 Constitution, if only by its recognition of the principle of universal suffrage, was a definite breach with the earlier Leninist concept of "collective democracy".[2] The Soviet Union has evolved its own way of life, and certain features of this will doubtless survive any change of regime. But no ideology is permanent, if only because it is not the practice of the young to accept without question the opinions of their parents, and thus as new generations grow to maturity the present

[1] Closely related to this concept is the invariable communist demand for a strong central government, responsible only to an "elected" popular Assembly, and the rejection of any form of federal government as less amenable to control. This again has been exemplified by the attitude adopted by the Russians towards the future political structure of Germany. But in their *Address to the Communist League* (March 1850) to the German workers Marx and Engels took precisely the same line. "The democrats will work either directly for a federative republic or, if they cannot avoid a single and indivisible republic, they will attempt to cripple the central government by the utmost possible autonomy for the communities and provinces. But the workers must not only strive for a single and indivisible republic, but within this republic for the most determined centralisation of power in the hands of the state authority." (S.W., I, p. 106.)

[2] Cp. Marx Vishniak, "Lenin's Democracy and Stalin's", *Foreign Affairs*, July, 1946, pp. 612 f.

ideology is likely to be modified. The process of change may be a slow one, and no one can foretell what form it will take. Yet it is most improbable that the rule of the party, as this was understood by Lenin and Stalin, will be unaffected by it.

Conclusion

The great reputation as a thinker that Marx enjoys today is largely due to Lenin. The October Revolution and the establishment of a soviet state naturally led to an increased interest in his teaching; and as soon as communist parties began to be formed, it became one of their duties to foster it by providing editions of his works, which were not readily accessible before 1917, with the exception of the *Communist Manifesto* and the first volume of *Capital*. Croce has referred to Labriola's difficulty in obtaining copies of the early philosophical writings, not all of which even Marx himself possessed.[1] His *Poverty of Philosophy*, the first attempt published in his lifetime to expound historical materialism, appeared in Paris in 1847, but it was only in 1896 that it was reprinted, and it was not translated into German until 1885 or into English until 1900. The *Critique of Political Economy*, with its celebrated preface, was published in a German edition of a thousand copies in 1859, but it did not appear in French until 1899 or in English until 1904. The *Critique of the Gotha Programme* (1885) was long withheld from the public, and when, at Engel's insistence, it was at last printed in 1891, it was buried away in the Viennese *Arbeiter-Zeitung*. It was not issued separately until 1920.

Engels tells us, however, that his *Anti-Dühring* (1878) was published in a "large edition", though how far it had a general circulation is another matter, as the German Government at once laid it under an interdict. According to Kautsky, however, it created the first Marxist school, and further German editions were called for in 1885 and 1894. Yet it was not translated into French until 1912 or

[1] See Marx to Engels, April 24, 1867, *Corresp.*, p. 217.

into English until 1935, and in those languages only such
sections of it were available as belonged to his earlier
Socialism: Utopian and Scientific, of which translations had
appeared. His *Origin of the Family* appealed to a wider
public, as anthropology was becoming fashionable; by
1891 it had reached a fourth edition and there had been
several translations of it. But Lenin recorded in 1902 that
his *Peasant War in Germany* had "long ago become a lit-
erary rarity", though a Polish translation, published in
London, had been issued in the previous year.[1]

But in social-democratic circles, particularly in Central Europe, Marxist ideas had a prodigious influence.
Such organs as *Neue Zeit* and the *Sozialdemokrat* assisted to
give them currency, and they were proclaimed by the
party leaders at their congresses. Thus, if we except England, "scientific socialism" was firmly entrenched by the
close of the century, and the more important of the
social-democratic parties had incorporated its principles
into their programmes. Lord Keynes has observed that it
"must always remain a portent to the historians of opinion—how a doctrine so illogical and dull can have exercised an influence over the minds of men, and through them
over the events of history".[2] Yet certainly there were many
who did not regard it as such. Its strength lay in its claim
to provide a total explanation of social phenomena, and
to do so in terms of an experience which the vast majority
share—that of having to produce in order to live; and
while it allowed the pundits scope for endless refinements,
it was fundamentally a simple explanation, the essentials
of which were within the grasp of anyone of ordinary
intelligence. Moreover, it gave the workers something
which none of Marx's precursors had been able to offer
them. They had been told often enough that their state
was a deplorable one, but this they knew already. What

[1] *What is to be Done?,* S.W., II, p. 48.
[2] *The End of Laissez-Faire,* 1926, p. 34.

Marx told them was that the very nature of the troubles they endured was a proof that their deliverance was at hand; and of this he claimed to provide a scientific demonstration by showing that, after passing through a number of historic phases, the productive forces had reached the point at which their inevitable further development depended upon their transference to the workers themselves, who would thereafter control them in their own interests.

Now Marxism, as we have seen, is a revolutionary creed. Marx does not indeed say explicitly that the new social order can only be achieved by a revolution. Yet he certainly implies it. For "the expropriation of the expropriators" and the transference of the means of production to the workers are not enough. The whole apparatus of the existing order—its legal system, army, police, etc.— must be swept away, and society be reconstituted upon entirely new foundations. This was what he meant when he said that the bourgeois state was to be destroyed, and that the workers were not to make use of any part of it. Those continental social-democratic parties which accepted Marxist programmes understood his doctrine in this sense, and were thus committed to destroying the bourgeois state and to setting up planned societies under proletarian dictatorships.

Marx's analysis of the capitalist system had led him to predict that while the exploiting class would contract ("One capitalist kills many"), the exploited class would proportionately expand and the lot of its members continually deteriorate. Hence it followed that the revolution would take place in the most advanced industrialised country, since it would be there that the conditions which created a revolutionary situation would first develop. But the predictions upon which this conclusion had rested had not been fulfilled. By the close of the century extensions of political rights and of social legislation, combined with the growth of organised labour, had undermined revolutionary Marxism in Western Europe, and it was only to a backward country, such as Russia, that its doctrines could still be applied. Thus, despite their programmes, it was inevitable that the social-democratic parties of the West should have been revolutionary only in name, and this was especially true of the German party, by far the largest and best organised of them all.[1] The power and wealth of Germany were increasing, her industrial workers were better off than they had ever been, and her governments were creating and extending social services. In such circumstances the destruction of the bourgeois state appeared utopian, and the leaders found themselves using their growing influence to obtain from it further concessions for the workers, and became persuaded that it was possible to take it over and convert it to proletarian purposes. Hence a contradiction arose between their revolutionary theory and their reformist practice. Yet it was one that they were unwilling to acknowledge. As Auer put it in a letter to Bernstein, "*Teurer Edi, das sagt man nicht, das tut man*".

But Bernstein, who had spent some years in London and had become acquainted with the Fabians, refused to accept this position. His criticism of it became known as "revisionism", and in current Soviet thinking this is so nearly identified with "reformism" that the *Short Philosophic Dictionary*, which devotes considerable attention to the latter, merely gives a cross-reference to the former. According to Lenin, reformism is "working for concessions from the ruling class, *not* for its destruction",[2] which was what the social-democratic parties were doing in one country after another, as Bernstein demanded that they should frankly admit. But in fact he went much further

[1] See John Plamenatz, "Deviations from Marxism", *Political Quarterly*, Jan.–March 1950, p. 42.
[2] *Can the Bolsheviks Retain State Power?*, Oct. 1917, S.W., VI, p. 277.

than this, and although he claimed that his "revision" of Marxism left its essentials unaffected, he not only challenged all its major conclusions, but also the dialectical method by which they had been reached.[1]

The opposition to revisionism was led by Kautsky, the pope of the German party and its leading theoretician. Yet when Lenin set up the revolutionary dictatorship of the proletariat, in accordance with Marx's teaching, Kautsky turned against him, and Lenin resented this the more as he had counted above all on the German social-democrats to lead the proletarian revolution in the West which was to come to the assistance of the new Soviet state. In the controversy that ensued, Lenin at least had the logic on his side. For a generation Kautsky had been regarded as the leader of revolutionary Marxism. While rejecting Blanquism, like others of his school, he had looked upon the revolution as the seizure of power by the proletariat, and had deprecated any weakening of the class struggle, or any tendency to disparage revolutionary action on the grounds that economic conditions were of themselves gradually bringing socialism into being. But when he saw these principles translated into action, he recoiled and took his stand upon parliamentary democracy, so that his final position became indistinguishable from that of Bernstein, with whom he became eventually reconciled; and it was he who was responsible for the "revised" Heidelberg Programme of September 1926, a profession of faith very different from the Erfurt Programme he had drafted thirty-four years before.[2]

How little revolutionary was the proletarian movement

---

[1] For the latest and most complete account of Bernstein's position see Peter Gay, *The Dilemma of Democratic Socialism*, Columbia University Press, 1952.
[2] Waldemar Gurian, *The Rise and Decline of Marxism*, 1938, p. 70; E. H. Carr, *The Bolshevik Revolution*, I, p. 239; F. J. C. Hearnshaw, *A Survey of Socialism*, 1928, p. 292.

in the years between Marx's death and 1914 became apparent when war was declared, and the leaders in the countries concerned supported their "bourgeois governments" and voted in favour of war credits. In so doing they followed the wishes of their rank and file. Marxism had indeed always condemned patriotism as an illusion fostered by the dominant class in its own interests. But this was now forgotten. The British and French socialists maintained that they were acting in accordance with their principles in resisting Prussian *Junkerthum*, and the Germans that they were upholding the same principles in opposing reactionary Tsarism. But Lenin brushed all this aside, and at the Zimmerwald Congress of September 1915, and with somewhat greater success at the Kienthal Congress of February 1916, he contended that the war was an imperialist one and should be converted into a revolutionary war, as Marx had prescribed. He found little support for this opinion at the time, but by the end of the war a reaction had set in, and a considerable section of the workers was prepared to endorse the view that the Second International had betrayed its principles. Thus in one country after another those who believed this broke away from the parent social-democratic parties and formed communist parties, which passed under the yoke of Moscow by affiliating to the Third International, founded by Lenin in March 1919. It was the parting of the ways. Had it not been for the war and the victory of the Bolsheviks in Russia, it is possible that the cleavage might not have taken place, but the two in conjunction made the contradiction between the theory and practice of the Second International one which could no longer be evaded.

Our judgement of the issue will depend upon our interpretation of Marxism. If the thesis that it is a revolutionary creed is correct, the leaders of the Second International, whom Lenin attacked, were not true Marxists, though they had been influenced by Marx, and had adopted many of his views. It may be urged that Marx's real concern was to remedy the lot of the workers, and that by the end of the century he would have been prepared to have admitted that this was more likely to be achieved by a reformist than by a revolutionary policy. But to have done so would have meant the abandonment of that theoretical analysis which distinguished his brand of socialism from all others. His case was that the collapse of the capitalist system was inevitable, and that it must lead to the establishment of a new economy under which alone the workers would obtain relief from their sufferings. It is scarcely thinkable that he would have been willing to renounce these conclusions for a position which he had spent his life in attacking. What is much more probable is that he would have recognised that the situation that arose in Russia in the opening years of the present century demanded a "narrow party", such as Lenin advocated, and that he would have approved the measures that the latter took to overthrow the Tsarist order and maintain his own.

That these measures should have led to state capitalism is not surprising. It was very well for Jaurès to declare that *"Le Socialisme n'est pas l'Étatisme"*, but no one has yet devised any workable system of the public ownership of the means of production which does not end by the state taking charge of them, as it (or rather the Communist Party which controls the state) has in Russia. It may be decided, for example, to base the new order on Co-operatives. But the essence of the Co-operative is that it is a voluntary association, and if everyone is to be obliged to belong to one, there must be some authority with sufficient powers to compel him to do so if he is unwilling. Or a Corporative system may be chosen, and every industry be represented in an economic parliament. But inevitably conflicts will arise between the claims of rival industries, and these can only be resolved by an authority powerful enough to enforce its decisions. In either case, we are thrown back upon the state.[1] It is significant that one result of the concentration of power, to which experiments in state capitalism has led, has been to rescue Proudhon from oblivion and exalt him to the position of a thinker of the first rank; though he never succeeded in showing how the loosely-knit communal organisation he favoured could be applied even to his own primarily agricultural country, let alone to one which was highly industrialised.

The transference of the means of production to public ownership and the planned society are of the essence of socialism. The difficulty has always been to reconcile the two, unless the first is to be understood in a purely formal sense; and the only group of western socialists squarely to face the issue were the Fabians who were state planners to a man and markedly undemocratic. What Lenin early came to see was that a nation-wide planned economy was incompatible with the parliamentary democracy of the West. If production is to be planned, some body of persons must do the planning, and this becomes impossible if the plan is liable to be reversed at any moment by a vote in a popular assembly. Under capitalism the planning is unconscious. It is not a perfect system, but if private enterprise is held, as it was by Marx, to be the cause of all social evils, so that its destruction possesses an absolute value, the only practicable alternative is state control, which is what Marx and Engels demand, though their theoretical objection to states prevented them from accepting it as a final solution. In this event, a state which desires to remain solvent may have to adopt such measures as the direction of labour, the fixing of wages and the prohibition of strikes, and take the necessary steps to

[1] Georges Bourgin and Pierre Rimbert, *Le Socialisme*, Paris, 1950, pp. 83–86.

enforce them. No Western democracy, based on universal suffrage, is likely to tolerate this, save in the emergency of war.

Had the West risen in rebellion, as Lenin and his associates believed in 1917 that it would do, Russia might well have remained an agricultural country, and have provided the granary of a socialist Eurasia.[1] When, by 1924, it had become clear that it was not yet ripe for revolution, Stalin embarked on his policy of building up Russia, of which "Socialism in one country" was the slogan; and it is reasonably certain that had Lenin lived he would have done the same. Now, thirty years later, Russia has her place among the great industrialised countries of the world. But this has only been achieved by intensifying the draconic discipline which Lenin and Trotsky had imposed upon all sections of society, and particularly upon the workers. Yet although Soviet policies have aroused the hostility of the West, all socialist parties have contained groups prepared to support or at least to condone them, as is only to be expected in view of the Marxist heritage which the socialists and the communists share. Of the Western parties, the British party has been least influenced by Marxism. None the less, the authors of *New Fabian Essays* and *Socialism. A New Statement of Principles*, both of which appeared in 1952, have felt it necessary to disavow elements which they admit to be specifically Marxist, such as "economic determinism", belief in the "inevitability of progress" in the sense of the inevitable evolution of society towards collectivism, and such notions as that "any collaboration between workers and employers is a betrayal of the class struggle" and that "the tolerance of a private sector of industry, however well controlled by the state, is a lapse from grace".[2] No

[1] Waldemar Gurian, *Communism, Theory and Practice*, 1932, p. 118.

[2] A number of German Social-Democrats have gone at least as far, to judge by the passages quoted from their writing, by the communist, Fred Oelsner in his *Der Marxismus der Gegenwart und seiner Kritiker*, Berlin, 1948.

workers' movement will be the worse for their disappearance, but until they have been officially repudiated by
socialist parties as a whole, there will be some grounds for
the charges that the communists bring against them.

For socialist opinion in the West is a spectrum which
shades off from the ultra-violet of a perfectly reasonable
desire to mitigate social inequalities to the infra-red of
communism without Moscow.[1] A re-statement of what
socialism means today would seem therefore to be desirable. The International Socialist Declaration of 1951 pro-
claims that "Socialists work . . . for a world in which the
development of the individual personality is the basis for
the further development of mankind", but this is a *cliché*,
and disingenuous at that, as it implies that the development of the human personality is a matter in which only
socialists take an interest. Historically, socialism stands
for a specific type of economic restructuring, based upon
a body of principles, to which Marx gave their classic
form, which postulates the collective ownership of the
means of production. Yet the attempt to achieve this has
given rise to so many problems as to impose upon those
who still make it their goal the obligation of showing how
it can be attained without destroying the freedom it professes to create.

Here at least the communists make clear where they
stand. They want a society in which private enterprise
will be abolished, and everyone will become the servant
of the state. In countries over which they are seeking to
obtain control, and where they have therefore to take
into account other left-wing, and even bourgeois, elements, they will indeed declare that they have no quarrel
with private enterprise as such, and intend only to nation-
alise certain public utilities and basic industries. It is
significant that when, in 1945, political parties were

---

[1] For a good summary of the various trends of opinion see Hans Jaeger,
"Die Weltsituation des Sozialismus", *Deutsche Rundschau*, March 1954, pp.
224–236.

allowed to re-form in the Eastern Zone of Germany, the economic programme of the communists was more moderate than that of the social-democrats; while in the period immediately following the setting up of the People's Republic, the writings of the Chinese Communist Party leaders expressed the most liberal sentiments, and declared that all the capitalist bourgeoisie had to fear was some measure of state regulation. But this trick has been played too often for anyone to be deceived by it. As soon as the communists are in the saddle, private enterprise is harried out of existence, though it may be found necessary, in the interests of increased production, to retain vestiges of it in the agricultural sector, as is the case in the Soviet Union even today. Thus "the expropriators are expropriated", as Marx and his socialist followers held that they should be. Until therefore international socialism defines in non-Marxist idiom the society it wants, and the methods by which it proposes to create it, its position *vis-à-vis* the communists will remain an ambiguous one.

Marx fought oppression and superstition wherever he believed they existed, and this must always be laid to his credit. Yet his principles have been of little benefit to those whom he sought to assist. It is easy enough to attack any economic system, as it is certain to contain features which are open to criticism, and to make large promises of replacing it by a new order of ideal harmony. But in an imperfect world no such order is attainable. "It is a disease of the soul", says a Grecian sage, "to be in love with impossible things." The removal of concrete evils is a more desirable objective than the pursuit of any abstract good; and as ideological revolutions never proceed according to plan, and are fated to lead to consequences which their authors had not foreseen, those countries must be accounted the most fortunate which contrive to resolve their problems by other and less desperate expedients.

INDEX